Talking to Angels

Other books by Robert Perkins

Against Straight Lines
Into the Great Solitude
Kamchatka/Land of Fire and Ice

Robert Perkins has made six films for the Public Broadcasting Service and for England's Channel 4. The films have won major awards and been shown widely in the United States and other countries.

Into the Great Solitude
Yankee in Kamchatka
One Man in a Boat
Home Waters
Talking to Angels
John Muir: The Wild Apostle

Copies of these documentaries on VHS may be obtained by writing:

The Char Press
18 Hawthorn Street
Cambridge, MA 02138

Talking to Angels

A Life Spent in High Latitudes

ROBERT PERKINS

Beacon Press

Boston

Beacon Press
25 Beacon Street
Boston, Massachusetts 02108-2892

Beacon Press books
are published under the auspices of
the Unitarian Universalist Association of Congregations.

00   99   98   97   96   6   5   4   3   2   1

Text design by Christopher Kuntze
Composition by Wilsted & Taylor
Photographs of *The Wedding Tree* by B. A. King
Constance by Albert Pinkham Ryder courtesy of the
Museum of Fine Arts, Boston (Abraham Shuman Fund)
Photograph of musk-oxen by James R. Abel
♾ Printed on acid-free paper

Library of Congress Cataloging-in-Publication Data

Perkins, Robert F.
    Talking to angels : a life spent in high latitudes / Robert Perkins.
      p.   cm.
    ISBN 0-8070-7078-5
    1. Perkins, Robert F.   2. Mentally ill—United States—Biography.
  3. Mackenzie (N.W.T.)—Description and travel.   I. Title.
  CT275.P5735A3   1996
  362.2′092—dc20
    [b]   95-46655

TO René

Unbeached Canoe

Emptied this evening
of the stuff of survival
for whom does it dance?

—James Merrill

Contents

Acknowledgments

I would like to thank the many friends who read the manuscript, whose comments improved its shape and form: Bob Finch and Kathy Shore, Tony and Judy King, Montgomery Goodale, Laurie Weisz, Larry Osgood, Tony and Whitney Oppersdorff, Sam P. Goodale, Lucretia Mali, Beekman and Elizabeth Pool, Andrew and Merrie Foley, Philip Frisbee, Mary Hooper, Michael Winston, Elsie Hull, and Dr. William Ackerly; my copy-editor, Marlowe Bergendoff; the Ingraham Merrill Foundation for its generous support; and the author (unknown to me) of the line of poetry that appears on page 106 for the joy it brought my love and me.

I offer special thanks to my editor, Deanne Urmy, a fellow traveler whose navigation made the difference between staying at sea and getting to port.

Talking to Angels

One

HuMpTy DuMpTy OcEaN

On April 5, 1968, Martin Luther King was shot to death. Also on that day, the largest military offensive to date was mounted against North Vietnam by South Vietnamese and American troops; President Lyndon Johnson had breakfast with former President Dwight D. Eisenhower on his way home from reassuring our Pacific allies that the war would soon be over; a new Volvo station wagon cost $3,800, and the most expensive suit advertised in that day's New York Times *cost $150.*

In the spring of 1968, I was nineteen and a freshman at Harvard College. I was soon to leave school, without even passing "GO" or finishing the year, to start a journey. A journey I have yet to complete.

The Ryder painting. At the museum.
Walking around the galleries, musing on the word . . .
U see Um. Muse Um. U use um.

The small boat in the tiny painting tilts toward me, a black oval adrift on a wine-dark sea. Something barely discernible is in the boat. Or someone.

In the painting, a moon hides behind cloud, its light diffuse, soft tears scattered on the water. No destination, no visible departure, only a small boat on open sea, at night, under a hidden moon.

Staring intently, I imagine myself in the painting: lean over the stern, hang facedown. Stare into the dark water to watch the marbled fire underwater: pale and green phosphorescence, white flickerings, stars made mobile and miniature, flung across multiple layers of water.

As I look up, the water's edge curls into the sky where the stars, gnat-size, immobile, repeat the water's pale fire. On my back in that boat, I inhabit both worlds, sea and sky, mobile and immobile, and imagine I am watching the surface of the water from underneath.

Inside the frame, the painting is tiny, like memory, no bigger than my two hands held up. The paint is thick and cracked, as though Ryder had wanted to create the waves themselves. He worked his canvasses relentlessly, but no matter how much he painted, he never got his waves to move. Whatever his soul touched turned to paint, still and quiet, almost eternal: a lin-seed Midas.

People call his paintings romantic. However, if you are there, outcome unclear, destination unknown, you would hardly call them—or the fear you feel—romantic.

I did not know I was talking out loud until a guard came toward me with a finger raised to his lips. I ran.

April 19, 1968. The FBI names James Earl Ray, an escaped convict, as the assassin of Martin Luther King. He is being sought under the alias of Eric Stavo Galt.

The ambulance: a dark tunnel ride and a siren's wail. Strapped to a stretcher inside, I hear it, not the way it would sound in the street, approaching and receding. This siren does not stop. One more thing telling me I have lost my keys. Still, a hard, small point inside me watches what happens.

Unstrapped from the stretcher, released from the straitjacket, placed in a chair in front of a young man in a suit, I squint. He appears behind a desk, at a distance. I squint again. Two big men, nervous in the face of my chaos, hover behind me. If I've died and gone to heaven, the Suit must be St. Peter and the other two, Angels. I say as much and start a joke about St. Peter and a groundhog. The Suit interrupts, "No. You're not in Heaven, and I'm not St. Peter. I am an admitting doctor at McLean Hospital. Something has happened to you and we're going to help you."

I say I do not want help. I say, if I've done something wrong, tell me and I'll undo it. The Suit keeps talking. His lips keep moving. I see his gestures, but too much havoc, too much waterfall sound fills my head for me to hear. He motions me nearer, holds out a pen, wants me to sign something. Fat chance.

I spit, or jump, or both. The Angels allow me no second chance. A sharp blow crumples me. Held by each elbow, I am led outside by the Angels, then into a tunnel. Alternately, I slump and go rigid. I don't want to go. As they carry me, the Angels joke to each other: "This is a Live One." One Angel's name is Turnkey. The other is a Mr. Shine. They take me to maximum security—Bowditch Hall.

May 24, 1968. Father Philip Berrigan receives a six-year prison sentence in a federal penitentiary for pouring ducks' blood over draft files at Baltimore's selective service headquarters. France is nearly paralyzed by student protests.

The Voices say, "Come out in the hall." They are the voices of my family and friends. They say, "This is an initiation. We can never say beforehand. Come out. It is your birthday. Come out of your room. Then we'll all leave."

If that's what they want, I'll do them one better. I take off the white hospital pajamas—cotton ones with a pullover top, a drawstring at the waist—and walk naked into the hall in my birthday suit.

Surprise.

No one I know is there. Only other people, dressed or in bathrobes and pajamas. I hear the sound of slippers shuffle across the floor. Nobody looks up, except a Blackman in a chair by my door. He stands when I walk out. Shorter than I am, he must be a Black Angel. We talk. He asks me if everything is all right. Takes my arm, walks me back into the room. I do not understand.

Says he wants me to put my pajamas back on. He holds open the bottoms. With a slow and deliberate motion, he ties the string at my waist. He gestures for me to bend forward so he can slip the pajama top over my head. As he slips the top over my head, my arms come to rest on his shoulders. He pulls away. I hold on. He twists. I hug. He yells. We fall, roll under the bed.

A host of Angels run in and pull us apart. They sit on me, call between themselves, "This is a Live One."

I am pinned facedown. A woman in white, who had stood at the side, leans near my face. She does not speak, shows me a needle. She disappears. I feel it in my ass. The Angels hold me until other kinds of hands take control, liquid water hands that sweep over me, knock me under like a wave at the beach, then pull me far out to sea.

Still aware in some half sense, but not awake, I feel them pick me up. The Angels are taking me somewhere. They place me on a table, a wooden one, in a white-tiled room that echoes. I am on my back. I see showers. They place my feet together. Many hands rock me side to side. They wrap me in something cool and damp. They place straps across this instant cocoon, one over my thighs, the other across my chest. Nothing of mine can move, except my head. I roll it side to side and stick my tongue out. I tell the Angels to fuck themselves.

June 6, 1968. Robert Kennedy is shot after a campaign appearance at the Ambassador Hotel in Los Angeles.

June 7, 1968. Sirhan Sirhan is indicted by a Los Angeles grand jury on a first-degree murder charge for the assassination of Senator Kennedy. On the same day, James Earl Ray is arrested in London; he had been traveling under the name of Ramon George Sneyd.

I am a small craft, cast off, floating on a sea of white tile. My horizon, a black line of tile halfway up the wall. White fluorescent light flickers around me. Adrift in a sea of white light. All sound sounds far off, even my screams. Don't know what to do. Watch the tiles. Part of me looks down on me saying that something awful has happened, what Noah would have said after the flood.

I see stars, blackness, and myself swimming into it.

Caught in a halfway world, I snap awake from something I felt, or dreamed, or dreamed I felt. Sweating. Terrified: a floating water sound mixing with sleep becomes confused with voices. I cannot breathe. A twist of the kaleidoscope, and images surface as my memory flickers.

My birthday. Not eating or sleeping for days. Walking all night through the city. See into people: their fears, their feelings, their thoughts. I tell them what I see. I am pulled a thousand directions, filled with a multitude of feelings, owning none. A cup for the world. Not one feeling lasts long before the next is thrown into me like more confetti. The only constant, the speed at which I change feelings.

I want to be taken care of.

I walk forty miles from Cambridge to home, even over the Mystic River Bridge. The house is locked. Sit on the porch while my parents sleep. The house, like a huge cat, purrs. I sit there, stare at the sky. The moonlight behind the clouds, a hidden Ryder moon, twists the clouds into human shapes: torsos, arms, legs, men, women tumble across heaven. In my head is a voice saying, "You have lost your keys."

In the morning, my parents are surprised to find me on the porch. They have no idea. I say nothing. They should know. My father has to leave for work. My mother looks worried, tells me to go lie down. I lie down on the bed, childhood memories floating around me. The room is not restful. I get up. Too much to do, but what exactly To Do?

I follow my mother around the house. She cleans. She does not know what to say. Or do. I leave. I go into the woods across the street from the house. I walk into the woods far enough not to see the house. I can hear car traffic, tires on pavement, occasionally a horn. The sound irritates me.

The woods are tall white pines and spruce. A few

bluejays move through the trees, calling. It is spring. The softer chirp of a robin nearby. Under my feet, pine needles make a small crunching noise. I hear my breathing. Sunlight filters through the needles on the spruces, the pines, striking parts of tree trunks, casting shadow on others.

I sit down. I look up. I see the cracked and ribbed bark of a pine, watch a steady flow of red ants move up and down the tree. They are comfortable, heads up or down. Why not me? The trees too seem satisfied. On the ground to my right, some lily of the valley. I crawl through them, drinking in the smell. A red squirrel jabbers, high up a tree.

I go over to a rock and knock on it. I lick it. I go to a pine and rub my body against the trunk. I sit perfectly still. Like Noah after his flood, I think I hear something, a sign. This time not the traffic. What?

I brush away pine needles and write in the dirt: rock, tree, needles, spider, lilies. As I turn from my list to the actual things, then look back at the list, the words convey nothing. I shrug, get up. Brush off the back of my pants. I need to be somewhere. I need to get out of here. I need to be taken care of. I leave for Cambridge.

I lie down beside the highway, sleep in the grass. The shoulder of the highway is soft. The cars swooshing by sound comforting. When I get up, the indentation in the grass looks as if an animal has slept there. I pass a lawn with a wire strung at knee level. When

I look at it, the wire begins to vibrate. Now, I have powers.

I change destination and return to my old school, a boarding school, an hour beyond Boston. This time I take the subway. Ride the SUB-way. Hear the same voices say, "You have lost your keys."

Go to the chaplain's house. His wife comes to the door, garden trowel in hand, welcomes me in and goes to find her husband.

Why am I here?

I pick up a newspaper. All the black-and-white words become black-and-white letters become black-and-white shapes become black-and-white chaos become I L L E G I B L E.

"Hello, Mr. Cleveland. Thought I would just . . . thought I'd come say . . . because I am leaving leveland, cleaving leaveland, because . . ." He tries to keep me quiet, to find out what happened, to get me to eat. In the evening, I take a bath. He puts me to sleep in his study on a cot.

Awake. The house is silent, asleep. Alone in the study, then I should study. I move to his desk, open a drawer, pull out a folder. Read a few sermons. Disagree with a few things, begin to correct his prose, adding a few paragraphs tentatively, then working faster, in a white heat. My words spill onto the desk, the walls. I write with a Magic Marker. Everything in the room becomes paper: the lamp shade, the calendar, the green desk blotter. I write on everything. I put the alarm clock in a drawer. I still hear it, the sound as soft as a kitten lapping milk. I work until dawn. There is the phone. I call home. The father answers; his first response:

"Where are you?"

I tell him how, when the sun wakes up, so does his son. Then I hang up. Go down the hall to wake up the Clevelands. Better yet, get into bed with them. Mr. Cleveland sits bolt upright.

"Go downstairs, wait in the kitchen," he says. In the kitchen, I wait. Terrified. Of what? Just terrified. . . .

June 8, 1968. At the funeral service for Robert Kennedy, his brother Edward recalls Bobby's saying many times, "Some men see things as they are and say, why; I dream things that never were and say, why not."

I flicker awake and find myself on a bare mattress in a blue, bare room. The Angels have returned me here from the white room. For the first time? Have they done this many times?

I think many times.

In the blue, bare room there is one large screened window looking outside, opposite a door with no door handle. In the door is a smaller, plastic rectangle of vertical window. Often, I see part of a face in the small window.

I have been somewhere else a long time. I hear, in the dusty way you hear things waking up, the heavy clunk in sand of something metal. Once in a while the clang of metal hitting metal. The sounds sound as if they are in the room, but there is nothing in the room but the blue, padded wall—and me on a bare mattress.

For the first time in a long time, I reconnect with something outside myself. What I hear are horseshoes being pitched. I lie perfectly still. Something tremendous has happened. What? To me? Scattered images and sensations rush through me uncut-and-all-at-once. I slide helpless back into that senseless ocean.

Awake again. A woman is talking to me. The same nurse kneels on the floor by the mattress. An Angel stands behind her watching. The woman offers me two small, white paper cups. Cups? The Queen of Cups? What is she saying? She touches me. I pretend not to see her, or hear her. They leave. Several Angels return with her. They hold me down. I cannot stop the woman from giving me the shot. Deep inside it stings, sits there like the larvae of some ugly fly. I sink again, but I did hear horseshoes.

August 8, 1968. At the Republican convention in Miami Beach, Richard M. Nixon is nominated for president on the first ballot.

To have the wind knocked out of you, hard, at nineteen. To give you the feeling of it, I'd hit you on the side of the head, when you were not expecting it, with a flat board or a piece of rubber tubing. The shock of the thing! Stunned, in pain, raging, you'd turn to fight, only to realize you held the crude weapon yourself.

I got out of the hospital after a year. I was lucky. Not that I was cured, as much as refolded. I tucked the edges of myself in enough to be allowed to live outside and hold a job. I worked in a bakery, in front of the big oven, putting in and pulling out loaves of bread, pastries, buns. I sweated a lot. The day began at 6 a.m. and ended at three. The baker worked me hard. He had no interest in my problems. I had plenty of time to think.

I was "recovering," and that's the right word. How accurate too with its suggestion that a return to life outside Bowditch meant covering up so much that I knew and felt. I got in the hospital because a gap developed between myself and the world, and I fell in. I could not see my face in the mirror because I had become the mirror. I had lost touch even with nature, replaced her with my own consciousness. I would have to learn all over again how to see her. Each day was an eon, as though another layer of sediment was settling over my soul, flattening my being and hiding it under a tremendous weight of ooze and sludge. Before I could pull myself back together, I would have to excavate. That's what I did after leaving Bowditch—I excavated. It was no surprise to me that once on the outside I preferred my own company and found some peace in nature. I did not notice my friends returning from Vietnam feeling any better about their experience than I felt about mine. Or treated any better by people who were not there. It took a long time to trust another person.

In the hospital I felt things, saw things that twisted

me. When I was in there, I needed help. What I didn't need was the help I got. I needed people who were not afraid, instead of Angels and doctors who talked at me as if I were an object. I learned to lie, to hide my feelings, to hate and not to trust. After I got out, my job was to stitch myself and the world back together. For too long I was attentive only to myself and trying to overhear myself, only to realize I was drowning the only voice I needed to hear—my own. But for years other voices only confused me. I hated it when friends and family felt sorry for me. I hated it more when I felt sorry for myself.

In the bakery, standing in front of the eight-foot-long oven, watching the shelves rotate inside, waiting to take bread out or put it in, I often thought of the desert and its heat. I thought of myself as a desert creature. At least looking out from my eyes, what I saw resembled desert. I prided myself on my leathery skin, on my ability to live on little water and to survive under rough conditions. I hid in the shade. For years, I lived carefully, certain that if I didn't control myself, I would be put back on maximum security, back on Bowditch.

They tell you at home and at school to be polite, well mannered, but they don't tell you where to put the rage. Like Mary who had the little lamb, everywhere I've gone the shadow of that year has been sure to follow. Where is the rage supposed to go, up the chimney like smoke, along with Santa Claus? Across continents to bomb the shit out of other people? Into the streets?

I might literally have gone south to the desert, but in my life I went north, to the tundra. Whenever I could afford it, I traveled into wilderness. I had the skills. It was good out there. I preferred the straightforward fear I felt and the physical dangers I faced to dealing with family and other people. Slowly, I stopped leaning on nature and began to just look, to see. She was all I could trust. That's the hospital's gift, the tight, hard seed in it: My world got boiled down so much that it became authentic. I would never have had the courage to travel alone, months at a time, if I hadn't been in the hospital. But it took a few years to appreciate this.

The nineteen-year-old in me still rages; the forty-six-year-old I am just shrugs. It's time they made peace. Even though it has taken decades, I no longer want to keep hauling that shadow around. That rocky year, nineteen, has haunted me long enough.

December 27, 1968. Apollo 8 astronauts return safely to earth after becoming the first men to orbit the moon.

I survived. Because of that hard seed, I bother to write. Maybe some poor bastard, one who's there now, or been there, or going to be in there, will read this and know that he or she is not alone. That the journey is worth taking, painful as it is.

With this as a motive, I want to re-enter that world through the three locked doors. Each one is opened and locked, opened and locked, and opened and locked behind me before I can enter, or leave, Bowditch. The TV room is to the left. It is always on. The nursing station is to the right. Patient rooms line the opposite wall. Between two of the rooms is a blackboard. I hate that board. Each of us has a number, a line all his own. The room numbers run down the left edge. Nurses and Angels write on the board in white chalk. Each day, I can tell by the handwriting if the Angel of the Board is a man or a woman. Loopy, cursive letters mean a woman. Next to your room number they write your name:

20. Perkins

There is space to say where you are. If you are off the hall, there is a box to put what time you left and, next to it, another to say what time you are expected back. There is a separate section headed "Outpatient" with a list of three or four "graduates" who come back to see the doctor occasionally. I went back after a year out to visit friends still on Bowditch and found my name listed under "Outpatient," as if they expected me anytime.

Opposite the board is a blank wall. Hot water pipes run close to the surface of that wall; it is always warm. I discover this watching one of the pacers, Jack. He always stops right there to rub his back against the wall like a cat. Jack is what we call a Double. He paces and, sliding hand or shoulder along the wall, keeps body contact with the building at all times. What terrifies him is to travel through space unsupported. To decide to cross an open doorway can take five minutes. When this happens, as he crosses open ground, he screams. He screams other times, too. That makes him a Triple. He paces *and* he touches walls *and* he screams at invisible voices. None of us can hear these, nor can we figure out from his replies the questions the voices ask him. His screams splinter into different voices, as if a whole city living in him is talking at once. We call him "Walking Tower of Babel," or "Tower" for short. Sometimes, for nothing better to do, a group of us join in like wolves and howl along. This upsets him, and he screams louder. An Angel comes out of the nursing station to yell at us to knock it off.

Walking past the nursing station, if I take a left, I face another door leading to the backyard. If I go straight ahead there are more rooms and, down a narrower hall, the bathroom and the shower room where they take us to put us in Packs. Packs are outlawed now, but they were a top-of-the-line restraining technique through the 1960s. It's what they put me in first. They can't wrap you in damp sheets and leave you in them for hours anymore. I've heard they don't need to now. There are new drugs that are more effective. Most times, I am so out of it when I am led down the hall I never know whether it is for Packs or a shower.

Toward the end of my year, I get to know a girl on another hall. Her name is Barbara. She is on Appleton. Appleton is heaven. I feel if I could only get there, my troubles would be over. I dream about Appleton. It is an open hall where patients can come and go as they please. They have many privileges. They can smoke and carry lighters. It is a mixed gender hall where patients have sex. So ran the rumor on Bowditch.

When I visit Barbara our conversations are not very deep or romantic; my Angel is sitting there beside us. We like each other. She tells me her story. She was a druggie. She lived in San Francisco at the height of it all: Haight Ashbury, love-ins, acid. One day, she dropped acid and went for a walk. She saw a slogan spray-painted on a wall, a big one, that read, "San Francisco Is Free." She thought that sounded right. Later in the day, she walked into a clothing store. She picked out a dress. She went into a changing room and put it on. She started to walk out of the store wearing the new dress, right past the cashier. She wasn't trying to steal it—"San Francisco Is Free." The lady at the register told her she had to pay for the dress.

"Is that right?" she said. "Can I wear it, if I pay for it?"

The woman at the register said, "Yes."

"Good," Barbara said. "I won't have it, thank you." She took the dress off, along with the rest of her clothes, and piled them on the counter, slowly. She walked out in the street because San Francisco, that day, was free. They locked her up. Her parents, who lived in the East, brought her back and put her in the hospital.

One day I call her up. The Angel answering the phone doesn't say, as they usually do, that he will get her. Instead, he says, "She is dead."

"Dead?" I ask.

He says, "Yes. Died in Packs. She was straining so hard she burst a blood vessel in her brain. She had an aneurism."

For a while, they give me the room next to the kitchen. After every meal, an Angel counts the silverware and throws the counted piece onto the ones already in the drawer. That's twenty times three pieces of silverware. How many clangs is that? Three times a day. If one piece is missing or they lose count, they count them again. If a piece is missing, the hall is shut down. No one can leave. All privileges are suspended. That way they figure the patients will help get that piece of silverware from whoever stole it. Most times, it is only misplaced, fallen behind something. We would spend days shut up for no reason.

One patient, Neal, loves the kitchen, loves to cook. He is huge and always laughing. He has supervised kitchen privileges at night. His specialty is French toast. Not any old French toast. If I am up, he cooks it for me. The bread is soaked in batter made from eggs, vanilla, sugar, a little milk. As one piece of bread soaks, the other is frying in butter. When it is fried, both sides, in goes the other one. The second piece is only fried on one side. He spreads jam on a side of the fully fried piece, then puts the fried side of the second piece on top of the jam and flips it over onto the uncooked side of bread. This keeps the double-decker French toast hot. He slides it on a plastic plate, pours syrup over it, eats it himself or offers it to me. On a good night he can polish off six.

When I left the hospital I weighed 240 pounds. I came in weighing 185. Eating and going to the bathroom are two things you have control over (most of the time) and get pleasure from doing. Neal was discharged before I left, and we learned soon afterward that he'd killed himself in Boston's Chinatown.

On Bowditch, we are our own entertainment. When Angels bring student trainees, part-time help, Young Angels in Training, onto the hall, usually the same four of us play a game. The trainees are young, no older than we are, and nervous. Here they are in a nuthouse for the first time, on a maximum security ward. They want to help, but they don't know what to expect. As the last door is locked behind them, we quietly spread out down the hall. First one, then two, then all of us begin to howl and roll on the floor, twitching and screaming about demons possessing our souls and how machines run the world. The Angels try to get us to knock it off. They apologize to the students, reassuring them that we aren't like this. They've seen us do this before. We babble louder. How are the students to know? Sometimes we keep it going for ten, even fifteen minutes. Our racket gets the real nut cases, the pacers, the screamers, the door-slammers going strong. When we stop, they carry on for real. Then we sit up and act ourselves, smile, and ask the students if they have a smoke.

Kim is the best, top dog. He has it figured out. He has it in his doctor's orders that they cannot give him drugs. He is smart. He's been in institutions for years, and he is only seventeen. He was locked up because he tried to kill his parents.

He would acquire enough privileges not to be watched closely, then he'd run away. On the outside, he does whatever he fucking well pleases until he is caught. When caught, wherever he is, he says, "Can't touch me, I'm a loony."

They ship him back to Bowditch, usually in handcuffs. When they bring him back, we all cheer and can't wait to hear the stories. How many cars stolen. How many chicks balled. That kind of stuff. We don't care if his stories are true, or not. We like to hear them.

Kim has a great stereo. When it's cranked up, the whole hall shakes. Because it's not legal to play music loudly on the hall, we gather in his room and pretend to be hanging out, talking. When Kim is ready to drop the needle on the record, we rush the door, lean on it, pile furniture against it. The louder the rock and roll, the better we like it: Jeff Beck, Dr. John, Janis Joplin, all of them. When the Angels finally break in, they confiscate the stereo.

Every time Kim returns from an escape, he is on two-on-ones for weeks, sometimes months. This means having two Angels no more than twenty feet away from him, night and day. Eventually, they have to reduce the guard to one. Then, Kim gets on group. He has no drugs in him. He can think. He uses all their rules against them. As soon as he sees the chance, he escapes again. What can they do?

We attend classes in the small school on the hospital grounds. This is all mostly a joke. The medications we are on make concentration difficult and reading impossible. The biology teacher is a determined woman who hopes to impart to us some of the wonders of the natural world. Earnest. She even begins making headway. To put a stop to this, Kim, who always sits in the back of the class, comes in with a copy of the *National Enquirer* hidden under his shirt. He raises his hand during class to ask if a woman can give birth to a pig. She says it is impossible, absolutely impossible. Kim stands up, brandishes the *National Enquirer* with the headline, "Woman Gives Birth to Pig Babies." We all begin to yell as the teacher chases Kim around the room, trying to get the paper away from him. Classes are suspended.

Bowditch was where Robert Lowell wrote his poem "Blue." That was when most of the patients were older and alcoholic. The young Boston University student mentioned in the poem is still here but not so young anymore. He makes a point of telling new patients about the poem.

While I was there Ann Sexton taught a poetry-writing class. She would come every two weeks to meet with a small group of aspiring poets. It was as boring a two hours as any other, although some of the students were entertaining. These wackos would rise to their feet and make up their poems right there, often yelling them out loud. A chorus of nutcakes. Occasionally, Ann Sexton would speak, but more often she sat there with the rest of us and let events swirl around her. If people wanted to argue about poetry or spout poems, that was fine with her. Most of us, and I was one, could barely raise our heads, let alone write poetry or find anything intelligent to say.

I've since come to appreciate how difficult it must have been for Ann Sexton to come back to the hospital and deal with a group of loonies. She had been there herself. Maybe she felt she could help one of us. Maybe she did. She chain-smoked through the sessions, making it hard to see her head sometimes. It helps me now to think of her there, but then the best part for me was the chance I had to smoke.

On the hall, I am not allowed to smoke. Too dangerous. I might burn myself, or somebody else. Having a lighter is an impossibility. The lighter of choice is a Zippo, a heavy steel job that makes a satisfying sound when you click it open or shut. The ritual of filling the lighter, pouring fluid into the cotton wadding, is only allowed to a few patients. The replacement of a flint, trying not to let the tiny spring slip out, is beyond most of us. Occasionally, an Angel lets me fill his lighter under close observation. On thorazine, smoking tastes terrible. The smoke turns your mouth into a sticky mess, the corners become dry, and small ridges of caked yellow crud gather there. Swallowing becomes difficult. We smoke as much as we can. It is a form of freedom.

I copy Kim once. The difference is that I never had escaped before, and I am heavily drugged. I decide that my best chance is on the way to the main cafeteria. We walk there from Bowditch in a group with only two Angels supervising. I could run into the woods, try to reach Route 128 and hitch a ride before I got caught. I dawdle at the back of the group. I wait until we are half-way between Bowditch and the main building before I sprint off. I head in the opposite direction from the woods to fool them. I lose the Angel chasing me by entering a building and slipping out a side door. I get to the woods without anyone behind me. I run fast. The highway is two miles away.

When a patient escapes there is an all-hospital alarm. Every Angel who is able joins the search. They either catch the patient quickly, or he or she gets away. Except for Kim, few patients get away.

Sooner than I expect, my whole body gives out. I've done nothing except eat and sit on a couch for half a year. I'll never make the highway. Instead, I circle back to the hospital at a trot. I walk through the parking lot to the wall of Bowditch's backyard, ease myself over it, drop the last eight feet. I walk up to the back door, ring the bell. The Angel who opens it looks surprised. He tells me I'm not supposed to be there. I'm supposed to be on escape.

Sometimes, new patients arrive in the night and are there on the hall the next day, like Christmas. Dr. C. arrived that way, except he came with a wheelchair because he had only one leg. He wears glasses and is overweight. At first, he is quiet. Sometimes they are like that. He watches what is going on, sizing it up through his thick glasses. You want to give that type a wide berth until you're sure what they are like. If you make a mistake, misjudge them and act friendly too quickly, they can bite your head off. Better to leave them to themselves.

He really was like Christmas for me, although I did not know it at first. In the same way hearing horseshoes being pitched helped me reconnect with the world, his arrival brought another level of healing.

On his third day, he has the balls to call me over. He tells me, doesn't even ask me, to go in and make his bed. He says he has a hard time with it because of the wheelchair. I could have told him to forget it or to get an Angel, but for some reason, I don't. Maybe he knew I would do it. I go in and make his bed. No big deal. An hour later, he is wheeling down the hall after me, saying the bed is not well made. It was true. I had done what we all do: throw the sheet and blanket over the mattress and drop the pillow near the head of the bed. I go back in and give it another try. He does not like that any better.

"What do you fucking want?" I yell at him, and he replies,

"A well-made bed."

So I do it. I really do it. I go in, strip the sucker, shake out the sheets, put on the bottom one, tight, then the top sheet, then the blanket, tuck them all in with hospital corners. I fluff the pillow and place it, gently, at the head of the bed. Dr. C. is watching. This time he says, "That is a well-made bed."

After that he expects me to do it every day. At first, I do not want to do it. Then I think, all right, I'll show the sucker. And I make his bed that way every day.

Dr. C. was a cancer researcher who lost a leg to cancer. What upset him, sent him here, was studying his own wasted leg. He took little interest in hall activities and avoided the politics and the fights. He sat on the hall during visiting hours. I never saw anyone with more visitors, mostly foreign young men and women. He conversed with them in many languages.

A couple of weeks after I start to make his bed, Dr. C. calls me over again. Guys in wheelchairs get used to bossing people around. He surprises me by asking what I know about the Greek alphabet. He takes out his pen and draws a few lines on a piece of paper, along with their English equivalents: Alpha, Beta, Gamma.

"What do you do with these?" I ask him.

"Nothing," he says. "Study them. Learn them. It might do you some good."

And it did, but not in the way he expected (or not the way I think he expected, but he was smart. He probably knew what he was doing). I couldn't care less about the Greek alphabet, but all of a sudden, trying to learn those stupid signs, I begin thinking about Greek myths. I had loved them as a kid. Read them in Bulfinch's *Mythology*. Now, I wanted to read them again. I went to

Ovid himself. The myth that hit home was about Narcissus. The beautiful part of the myth is the ending. How he finally connects with the world. How he joins himself by slipping into the water, but before he does, he calls to the trees. After he does, he is transformed into a piece of nature, a flower.

April 3, 1969. Vietnam: U.S. deaths reach 33,641, passing the total number of Americans killed in the Korean War.

Thorazine knocks the shit out of you. You cannot think straight. Your mouth feels like cotton. Your eyes don't focus. Sludge runs through your veins. To counteract the side effects, they give you Stellazine, but Stellazine has side effects, so they give you Cogentine to deal with Stellazine's side effects. The medications steal your energy. Several minutes of anything physical, except eating, exhausts you. You cannot read. You get lost, as in thick smoke. When the doctor asks you if you have any requests, and you say you want off the Thorazine, he tells you, politely, he cannot do that. That is your medication.

I had no chance of getting better until I got off that crap. Even when I was off it, years went by before it left my body. The habit, the effects, the residue of it stay with you. Each passing year, I would feel stronger, only to realize the next year I had more energy to get back.

May 5, 1969. The Boston Celtics win the NBA title for the eleventh time.

Every twenty minutes, night and day, an Angel checks on you. If it's nighttime, and you are trying to sleep, they flip on the light and look through that small rectangle in the door. I only see part of their face. Every twenty minutes.

I would have been happy to maim Angels. To kill them would have been too kind. I did get one. His name was Charles—not Charlie, but "Charles"—Godell. I am convinced the Angels did not use their real names. Many were metaphorical: Mr. Shine, Mr. Turnkey, Mr. Hope. That was smart. Makes it harder to look them up in the phone book later, in case an angry Nut-O wants to get together and talk about old times on the hall.

Godell got too close. As though he were blind, he would stuff his face inches from yours, then ask how you were feeling. How do you think I feel, you prick, when you've got your face and bad breath in my puss. If you told him how you really felt, he would write you up in his notes as showing aggression. So, you backed away saying nothing much.

I am sitting on the hall couch, across from the kitchen. "Charles" opens the kitchen door. He goes in and gets two cups of coffee. He is coming out when a patient walks up and asks for a coffee, too. The rule is: if the kitchen door is open and a patient asks for coffee, the Angel has to get it for him. Godell looks at the patient and gently shoves the door shut with his foot (I hear the lock catch). As the door shuts, Godell says to the patient, "Sorry, as you can see, the door is shut."

They stand there glaring at each other. I can see the patient is upset, but he turns away. After "Charles" starts to turn away, the patient whips around and nails him, spilling hot coffee over them both. They roll on the floor, the patient punching the shit out of Godell. The patient is only a little guy. They drag him to solitary, kicking and screaming his little heart out. When Godell stands up, he says he has no idea what came over the patient. He says he cannot understand it. I wanted to join the patient in kicking the shit out of Godell. But I neither join in nor call Godell a liar. On the hall, Angels are always right.

At the time, I had an unusual privilege. I asked for it after half a year and, miraculously to me, it was granted. I was allowed to split wood for forty minutes, twice a week. My old man brought in his wedges and sledgehammer, and I went at it. It is physical. It gets me moving, gets me outside.

While it lasts, I go to the woods for forty minutes twice a week. Shortly after Godell screwed the patient, he was assigned to be my Angel while I split wood. "Charles" takes me out there; sits down to watch. He cannot get close to me, or talk to me. I am working. Often, I stop to rest. Deliberately, I pick twigs and chew them, even as I work. I notice Godell picks one off a bush and starts chewing it. Maybe he does it because he sees me do it. Maybe not. I see the kind of twig he is chewing. What I can take credit for is not telling him what type of twig it is: poison sumac. After forty minutes, we go back in the hall, and that's the last we see of "Charles" for three weeks. When he comes back on the hall, he still has scabs on his lips. He had not been able to swallow, or to eat or drink anything for a week. He had poison sumac on his lips, in his mouth, and down his throat. Of course, I tell the patient as soon as he is out of solitary. He gets a kick out of it, and he keeps it quiet, too. He knows Godell will get me if he thinks I knew. Godell has his suspicions, but he can't prove them. Even when everybody on the hall starts to congratulate me, I just keep saying I had no idea.

When I am thirteen or fourteen I go out to see a movie with some friends. They are older. They have the car. My old man sees me leaving the house in a blue-jean jacket. He says, "And where do you think you are going dressed like that?" I tell him to the movies. He says, "No you are not. You put on a coat and tie." I tell him I won't do it. We have a yelling match, but I wind up leaving in a coat and tie. I wasn't even smart enough to say, sure, fine, and then ditch the coat and tie outside, like my older sister said I should have done. I'm either too much like him or too sensitive to his criticism, or both.

I can still see him soon after they admitted me, bumping his back against the wall, looking around with his little boy look, saying to me, "Do what they say. They know best." But he got to go home that night.

May 15, 1969. From New York to California, students are occupying college campuses to protest the Vietnam War. Police disperse a Berkeley anti-war demonstration with shotguns and tear gas.

Navigation is the art of going from what you know to what you don't know. The hall is named after Nathaniel Bowditch, another rigid man, the father of navigation. For centuries ships depended on his system. They went around the world on it, across oceans. For all I know, NASA sends up their rockets with his knowledge. It's all math and rational. There are many ways to navigate, but even knowing how doesn't necessarily keep you off the rocks. The man went nuts. His family locked him up in McLean Hospital. Later, they named the maximum security hall after him. There is a statue of him in Mount Auburn Cemetery holding a globe and a sextant in his lap. There is also a waiting list to get into both places, Bowditch and Mount Auburn Cemetery.

What got me there? No one but myself. Or is that true? A paradox. All to safely say is we start in the same boat. Most people stay in the boat. They are terrified not to. A few are pushed out. Fewer leap into the sea. Is being in the boat better than being in the sea? Survive either one, you might learn a few things. You could become amphibious—like a toad.

Near the end of my time on Bowditch, I was transferred to the corner room, a quieter room away from hall noise, next to the one where Dr. C. had been. This room had two windows that looked out, not at the backyard, or the parking lot, but woods. The same woods I had split wood in, where Godell had chewed poison sumac—a tangle of young maples, oaks, a few birch, some spruce.

Soon, I would be out.

Ferns were unfurling above last year's brown leaves. Red buds on the maples popped into soft, miniature leaves. I stood hours at the window wanting to see it actually happen, but like trying to see myself blink in a mirror, I could not. Neither could I hear the new leaves rub together, but I could imagine it, almost taste it: a velvet, soft thing, the way swallows' wings sound, not the brittle, dry rasp of fall leaves.

I would get out soon.

One afternoon, outside the window, the air filled with white floating flakes. Finally, I saw they were coming off the spruce trees. They were the tiny, transparent, light brown bud-caps that hold the new needles until the needles are long enough to launch these wafer-thin offerings. All the evergreens were launching them. In the sunlight, they looked white, like snow.

Some nights, I swear, I could hear the growing. I

would be standing at the window, or lying in bed in the dark between checks, and hear it above the smack of counting silverware or the outbursts of other patients; even see it, that free, unjudging green world growing, just the other side of that wall.

"M" *is for* Musk-Ox

Kafka said that to discover the whole universe he did not have to leave his room, not even his desk. He could sit still, close his eyes, and the universe revealed itself to him. . . . It could not stop itself from rolling in ecstasy at his feet. That has not been true for me. I have had to leave home, go out into the world, and then it's been me, not the universe, that cannot stop from rolling, and not always in ecstasy.

I did live in a meat locker for two months—something Kafka would have appreciated—at the western edge of the District of Mackenzie, near the Thelon Game Preserve in the heart of the Canadian Northwest Territories. The meat locker was on the bank of a great northern river, tributary to the Back, called the Baillie. The tundra.

Someone in Water Survey, a department of Environment Canada, was visiting the States when he saw a meat locker and had the vision of using it as a cabin in the arctic. He called the manufacturer and asked if they could cut windows in the sides of a locker. They said they could.

My job was reporting the weather for this part of the middle arctic. Twice a day I called in my observations on a small battery-operated, orange radio. It needed lots of antennae, set as high as possible above ground, to reach the several hundred miles back to Yellowknife.

There are no trees in the tundra. To achieve the height I needed for the antennae, I climbed on top of the meat locker and tied two old caribou antlers to either side of the roof, then strung the antenna wire between them. Looked at from the front, or back, the meat locker could be imagined as a boxy kind of caribou, twelve feet high.

My meat locker was big enough for two bunks, a table, and a sink. It was just tall enough to stand up in. What makes a meat locker suited to the tundra is its insulation. In the summer the locker stays cool, and in the winter it retains its heat. It comes ready-made. All you do is build a platform and screw the parts together. In the opinion of the Water Survey, this was an improvement over the older way of building cabins out of wood.

My friends at Water Survey left it for me to figure out it was a meat locker. They referred to it lovingly as their "research station" or "cabin." They said I could use it if I reported the weather, and if I brought a gun. Being the weatherman meant calling in twice a day. The gun was in case of a bear attack. I suspect they wanted to keep an eye on me, to be sure I was all right. If the gun did not work and I did not report in, they would come looking for me.

"Let's hope," someone from Water Survey said cheerfully over coffee, "we get there soon enough to find enough of you to send home."

Having been given the job, I wanted to do it right. I was terribly nervous until I talked to my expediter. Expediting companies are the voice of civilization for bush camps. They get food orders ready, find needed spare parts, handle emergencies, and often just talk to the people out in the camps to keep them sane. For the large bush camps they service, they buy supplies in bulk. I was able to piggyback on their camp orders and buy my supplies cheap.

My expediter, Jean Buck, was of the old school. When I told her I had no prior experience, she said not to worry. She gave me a pamphlet on weather terminology and definitions: what a cumulus cloud is, how to describe the force of the wind, that type of thing. Then she told me nobody would be interested in my weather reports. She said any pilot flying my way would know that the weather would have changed by the time they passed by.

She said she'd had the same job once and would lie in

her bunk and make it up. She said everyone did that, if they felt lazy. What they really want to know, she said, is that you are all right, and whether it is a bad day, or a good day. They will come and get you, she warned, if you start reporting UFOs and tornadoes. Much relieved, I left.

I flew out of Yellowknife weeks ahead of the thaw. There is a period of transition between the arctic winter and spring when planes cannot land on the tundra with skis. I could have waited to go in until the rivers and lakes were ice free and the plane could land on floats in water, but I wanted to be there in time to see the breakup of a great northern river. We took off with months of food stacked in cardboard boxes behind the cockpit. My friends had said the plane could taxi right up to the door of the cabin. With that thought in mind, I had not bothered to repack the boxes.

At the first sign of snow flurries, the pilot was ready to go back. He was new at his job, too, and was terrified of losing eye contact with the ground. I could see his point. We traveled for half an hour through snow and could not see a thing. If there had been mountains around, or if we had been trying to land, we would have been in trouble.

Luckily, the snow stopped as we reached the Baillie River.

We could not find the cabin, let alone taxi up to the door. I had a map of where it should be, and my Water Survey friends had said to look for the bright red fuel barrels with the yellow stripe. From hundreds of feet up in the air everything below us looked white.

Ready to give up, the pilot spotted one barrel that was not covered with snow and next to it, the cabin. He circled the spot many times looking for a place where he felt comfortable landing. He chose a lake behind the cabin. From the air, the lake looked close to the cabin. From the ground, it was a good half mile away.

We climbed out on mushy ice. The pilot said I was lucky I hadn't waited a few more days. The ice would have been too soft. As he was filling up the wing tanks with fuel for his return flight, I casually asked about taxiing over to the cabin.

He already thought I was nuts to come here alone for several months. He had told me so. Now, he was polite enough not to tell me what he was thinking. He just pointed to the clouds, as if they were his answer. He said it could snow any minute. He helped me pile the boxes of food and the duffels of gear on the ice before he took off. As the noise of the engine died away, it did start to snow.

I picked up a box and headed for the cabin. The snow had a crust on top of it not quite thick enough to hold my weight. Each time I broke through the crust, there was no telling how far down I would sink. One step and my foot would go down six inches. Five steps later, I would pitch forward as my foot went in several feet, the drift up to my crotch. I learned quickly to walk the long way around the drifts and try to stay on the ridges.

I had the key to the cabin door in my pocket. Before I could use the key, I found myself looking at a six-foot-high snowdrift blocking the door. My gloves were back among the pile of stuff on the ice. If there was a shovel, it was inside the cabin.

With the snow starting, the thought that I could not get into the cabin terrified me. There I would be when they found me, frozen to the ground after the worst spring blizzard in memory . . . and I had not even called in to report it.

I found a board at the side of the cabin. The snow was not ice, and I shoveled in a frenzy until the board snapped. With the shorter piece of board, I finished the job.

The lock was frozen. I could not get the key in it. The two windows, one on either side of the odd-looking cabin, had protective steel grills welded over them. I had to get in through the door. I went back to the boxes piled on the ice and dug out my gloves and a lighter. After I realized that heating up the key worked better than trying to heat the lock, I got the door open.

Inside, blown through cracks, there were more snowdrifts. Eventually, I got the heater going. By the time it was dark, I had brought most of the boxes to the cabin. There were a few left on the ice, but they could wait.

I decided to have my revenge by making the snow work for me. I left the cases of beer and sodas outside, along with a case of hotdogs and a case of hamburgers.

In the morning, because they had frozen, the cans had exploded their tops. Wolf tracks around the cabin told me where half my meat had gone.

Over the next two weeks, the snow began to melt. My spirits, along with the weather, improved. The first creature I saw through the binoculars was a wolverine a half mile off, bounding fast out of the valley, a dark spot against the snow. All I had done was open the cabin door.

Patches of brown tundra began to appear. I did not hold a grudge against the wolves for eating my meat. I would have done the same. In fact, the wolf and its mate were friendly enough to include the cabin on their daily rounds. As the landscape gained color, I looked forward to seeing their two white shapes drift across the landscape.

I saw the first bird when I brought a pail of food scraps out of the meat locker and dumped it on the ice in the middle of the still solidly frozen river. Twenty minutes later a raven flew over. Five minutes after that half a dozen seagulls landed and devoured the garbage.

As the weather improved, the migrants appeared: little sparrows, snow buntings, loons, and skeins of geese —all proclaiming spring with their song. On quiet days, even though they flew by high up, I could hear the odd zinging of the goose wings fanning the air on the downbeat. The snow geese flew with the Canadas. The laughing geese did, too, and occasionally mixed in among them were pairs of sandhill cranes, different in voice and large in shape beside their companions.

I found more tracks on my walks: rabbits, foxes, ground squirrels, mice, and even bear tracks. The area around the cabin was sandy, good denning for all the mammals.

Everyone was hunting. One thing I could tell they were getting were ptarmigan. Along with the ground squirrel, or siksik, the ptarmigan has the dubious distinction of being near the bottom rung of the food chain. Early on, I had seen many ptarmigan whirring up from the snow. They were white then. Unfortunately, they remained white as the land turned brown and became an easy target for predators. On walks, I would find starbursts of white feathers scattered on the ground, as though the bird had exploded. I suspected an owl I caught sight of in the neighborhood, but it could have been any number of other birds or animals.

The river beside the cabin became more like a creature itself. Every day I heard it stretching, groaning, gurgling, fed by countless ribbons of small streams as well as bigger, louder ones. Up until the first week in June, I could stand on the river's icy back. From its middle, I had to look up forty feet to see the edges of the banks. After the first week of June, it was too risky to go down on the ice. Deep cracks showed, and in places water lay several inches deep. Instead of a white, snow-covered expanse, hues of green and blue appeared.

The river broke open on the twelfth of June, and ran havoc for a week. At first, I heard only more bluster and noise. Then small advance wedges of ice thrust up, skidding across the still frozen center. More water, more noise, more buckling; the water swelling up from underneath the resisting ice until, in great screams and bone-cracking snaps, the ice gave way. It was hard to imagine that the river had been recently a walkable highway or that it would become liquid and calm enough to paddle down.

Chunks of ice carried boulders, rocks, and dirt. There were blocks thrust onto the bank by more ice behind them, then knocked back into the river by other pieces of ice. Weeks after the breakup subsided, I would find bergs twenty to fifty yards inland from the bank, marooned whales of slowly melting ice. Even stranger was finding huge rocks with skid marks behind them, as if they were monstrous, snail-like creatures. The river ice had pushed higher and farther inland, moving anything in its path, even huge boulders. Stranger still was simply finding skid marks running inland, made by icebergs before they melted, giving the impression that the snail-like boulders had flown off, the way I've found bird's footprints in the sand that simply end, beside them a delicate scrape remarking where the wing had pushed off.

At its height, the ice towered over the banks, reaching inland with its grinding, rubbing, and crushing. A week after it began, it was over. The water remained high, running fast, but the ice had passed. Occasional floes held back in an eddy floated by, but they were silent.

I met a bear during my stay. I was sitting at the table looking out the window on the river side of the cabin. Behind me was the sink, a basin with a length of plastic tube that went from it through the floor and stopped six inches above the ground, two feet in from the side of the cabin. Everything drained there, all the scraps and bits of food.

First there was a tremor, like the beginning of an earthquake. Then came a solid thumping as the side of the meat locker was raised slightly and fell back. This happened several times. The bear was having difficulty reaching under the cabin to the food scraps that had spilled out the drain.

I was safe enough inside. The walls were six inches thick and the grillwork was substantial, but bears are smart. Like the gray squirrels I was used to, bears like a challenge. Maybe it had a welding torch. I went over to the window where I could watch. I yelled at it to go away, but it did not seem to hear me.

The frustrating thing about the cabin was that I could not see the bear after it left the sinkhole, unless I went out the door. That I was not going to do. For all I knew the bear's attempts to reach the sink droppings were only a feint. What he really wanted was for me to open the door and step out.

I listened at the walls. I listened hard, my ear against the door, for heavy breathing. I hoped it was not the Gary Larson cartoon kind of bear that knows tricks, like holding its breath.

Armed with the shotgun the Water Survey had given me, I opened the door and fired a round into the air. Hours later, when I stepped outside, there was no bear. It probably had not been there for hours. After that, I took the gun on my walks, which was unfortunate because when you carry a gun, you begin to think like it. I never saw the bear again.

On one of my last walks at the cabin, on a hot day with white puffy clouds stuck in a china blue sky, I came across a haunting sight.

I was following the game trails along the side of the river. Game trails are lines of thought; they meander, crisscross each other, and flow off in odd directions. When I first arrived, I did not follow them or see this. On days when there was little wind and the bugs were bad, I would be in a hurry to get where I was going and would cut across them. There are thousands of trails in each square mile of tundra. Looking down from a plane, I could hardly believe there were so many. As I became accustomed to following them—some were deep ruts—I felt more connected to my neighbors who made them. The main trailmakers are migrating caribou, but paths are made by the whole range of tundra animals—voles, siksik, foxes, wolverines, musk-ox.

On this day, if I kept moving, the bugs were not so bad. I followed a trail and discovered a small stream where I surprised two big trout. It was a risk for the big trout to come up the small, shallow stream. The wealth of easy bugs and minnows to feed on must have been worth the risk. In the narrow stream, the fish had a hard time turning around. When they saw my shadow they made big splashes trying to get to deeper water.

Picking my head up from a daydream, I saw a lone caribou standing up to its belly in the river, gazing raptly at the opposite bank. It could not see me. I crouched. It was watching for something. We both waited. Nothing happened. A lone caribou, standing stiff-legged in the river. I was puzzled.

The caribou came ashore, wading the last yards in to the hard clay bank. Whatever it had been waiting for seemed to have left. The caribou lowered its head and spread its front legs to reach tufts of grass on the hard sandy beach. In that moment, a wolf barreled out of the dunes. The caribou spooked. All its legs jumped out at once, propelling it back into the river. The wolf followed.

The caribou swam across the river faster than the wolf. The current was swift, and they both had to work hard. The wolf fell a hundred yards behind.

Out on the other side, the caribou turned to watch

the wolf, then jogged fifty yards upstream, nearer to me. Getting out of the water, the wolf ignored the caribou, shook itself, and headed inland. The caribou did not move. It kept its eyes focused on the dunes where the wolf had disappeared.

I could see them both. The wolf went behind the first dune and lay down in the sun. It curled up and went to sleep. The caribou stood next to the river, tense and ready to jump back in. I would have moved closer, but I didn't want to scare either animal. The caribou and I waited for the wolf. If there had been two wolves, we might not have been waiting.

Three more times over the course of four hours, the wolf pursued the caribou across the river. Each time it lost the race and disappeared to rest. The caribou was three or four years old and in good shape. If wolves are opportunists, as I have been told, this seemed like a lot of work. I wanted to see how this would play out. I had switched sides. At first, I was for the caribou. Now, I was rooting for the wolf. If he won, I would get a steak.

While I waited, for some odd reason I remembered an intriguing definition from Simone Weil. When I first heard it, it had seemed cold: "Love is the giving of attention to an object." What was present in this riveted attention? What eternal energy? From the first day the wolf and the caribou locked eyes, they had been in this dance.

The caribou led the wolf across the river one more time, to my side. Then it took off, not waiting for the wolf. The wolf did not rest but ran after the caribou. I stood up and we all ran inland, the caribou leading. I soon lost my breath and had to stop, while the others became smaller and smaller before they disappeared altogether. I walked back to the cabin, the image of the wolf and the caribou now only in my mind, in miniature.

They are still there, in miniature.

Two weeks later, I put away my heaviest clothes, packed my camping gear, left my metal and plastic garbage—including the radio and the gun, and anything else I didn't need—in the cabin and launched my small canoe, Loon, into the Baillie River. No more weather reporting. The meat locker disappeared behind the first bend. It felt good to be a nomad and on the move.

I gave myself more than enough time to canoe the lower half of the Back River. I had been there before, but I did not know it well. Overconfidence kills more wilderness travelers than bears.

I have noticed that over the years my trips have become longer in time and shorter in distance. I had forty days to paddle a couple of hundred miles. When I was younger, in my twenties, I paddled with my partners or on my own twenty-five, thirty miles in a good day and thought little of it. Nor did I think then of what I might have missed.

What I looked forward to this season was trying

something new: walking away from the river. Canoeists in the arctic do not wander far from their route. Part of this comes from being a visitor in an immense and untamed landscape. Not to have a set course and a strict timetable is to invoke images of sloth—and also danger. Winter is never far away; violent storms can begin as early as August. It is easier to remember obligations back home and keep moving than to inspect your fear and linger with it among unusual surroundings.

Your constant companion is fear nevertheless, especially traveling alone, months at a time. It haunts you. My worst fear is that I might die out here. No, that's not quite right. A worse fear is that I might die slowly out here. For encouragement, I often think of the traditional Inuit who lived in the tundra year in and year out for centuries. For them the tundra was one big river, a river of life. They moved around from one location to another, depending on the season and on what they needed or hoped to get.

On my first four-day hike away from the river, I picked a long esker, high up with a good view of the surrounding country, made mostly of hard-packed sand. On the first night, I camped five miles inland.

The next day I was down among the rocks again, walking toward a small hill with what looks like an Inukshuk on top. Inukshuit are the totems the Inuit set up. Everyone has a theory about them: they were for blinds; they were to herd caribou; they were for navigation. They were to string line between for drying fish or meat. They were set up for friendship; they were perhaps astronomical sites. I bet there are reasons, too, that nobody has guessed.

I prefer the old Inukshuit, not those set up by modern-day canoeists. The new ones tend to be overbuilt. The older ones are more simply constructed, covered in lichen at the connecting spots. It takes a long time to grow a good lichen.

I was sure I was walking toward a classic Inukshuk. This far away from the river, it had to be authentic. At the top of the hill, I knelt to inspect it. Even though the totem stood out clearly from a distance, it was only two feet high—three stones leaned against one another forming a little structure. I was sure there was something inside, a secret. I carefully took the rocks apart. There was nothing there. I sat back on my haunches and laughed. That was the secret. I put the three rocks back together the way I had found them, still chuckling.

It sounds contradictory, but I do not mind meeting people on the river when I am alone. I have learned a lot from seeing how other people travel. On one trip, I met another solo canoeist, a medical student from Ohio, taking several months off. We spent an evening together. I watched him set up his small tent by crawling inside to fasten the tent poles. A million mosquitoes and black flies went in with him. When he backed out, the bugs stayed in the tent. He didn't seem to care. I thought he must have a secret I did not know. I casually asked him what he carried to deal with the bugs. Nothing, he said. He had heard they were so bad that nothing helped. I was impressed. I carry bug dope, and I use it liberally, and I have a headnet to wear on the worst days. Here was someone who carried nothing!

Later, he asked me what I had for bear protection. At the time I carried a whistle around my neck, and I had a few M-80 firecrackers. He showed me what he carried—a hefty .44 magnum handgun, the kind of weapon Clint Eastwood wields. He said his dilemma was that if he fired it, he would lose part of his hearing, the gun was so loud. We were both polite and did not say the other was a fool, but we thought it.

This summer, I met two men from Ireland. They said the landscape reminded them of home, only it was bigger, lonelier. In Ireland, they got backing from different companies by promoting the trip as a "first time white man ever set foot there" type of heroic adventure. They said there was a group of teenage girls behind them. They could not tell their sponsors that a group of six teenage girls had passed them on the river. They were paddling hard.

However, I thought I should look into this. The Irish lads said the women were a half day behind. I camped on the left side of the river, where the Consul River joins the Back. By the next afternoon I had everything ready.

I popped a pot of popcorn and prepared a thermos of hot soup. I had three candy bars left. I had turned Loon on her side, bottom facing the river, and taped my sign to the bottom. It read:

Hot Drinks, Popcorn, Candy, 5 cents.

I set up a seat next to the canoe, got out my book, and waited. Several hours later, I saw them turn the corner. Like a good wolf, I pretended to be asleep. When they paddled up, they yelled from offshore,

"Are you all right?"

I waved them in. They thought my sign was a hole in the canoe and that I was in distress. When they were close enough to read the sign, they broke into giggles. At first, they fished in their pockets, thinking I wanted the five cents, and asked if I did this all the time. I thought they meant operate a concession stand, and I said, "I would like to, but business has been very slow. I'm thinking of giving it up." They were young. It all made me feel old.

They ate the popcorn, ate the candy bars, drank the soup, and left me sooner than I would have liked. They were a camp group from Minnesota, girls between sixteen and eighteen. The counselor was twenty-two. Their camp ran senior trips in the tundra all the time.

Every season has its silence. In the tundra, if you are lucky, you can experience three seasons in two months: spring, summer, and fall. It was mid-July now, deep summer. Dust and pollen hung in the air, and the floating heat made the earth shimmer, as if it would float away. A hum, maybe caused by the thousands of tiny wings, the flowers, the rich tapestry of life, seemed suspended in this heat. The tremendous energy of nature's loving indifference swallowed Loon. And me with her.

I was anxious entering the big lakes. There are four of them in a row: Pelly, Upper Garry, Garry, and Lower Garry, Garry being the biggest. I do not like crossing large bodies of open water in a small canoe. If the weather changes during the crossing, I can get hammered. Without leaving shore, plain bad weather can lock me in. I am vulnerable. I thought about being tipped over in a freak storm too far from shore to save myself.

Canoeists worry constantly about things that can happen, it's an addiction. Here I was twenty miles this side of the big lakes on a perfectly calm, sunny day, already a floating corpse, or at least windbound for a week. I remembered to say, "thinking." I have learned to say this to catch myself from getting too worked up. I say it and, if I am lucky, let go of the obsessive thought and return to the present.

The water was sheer. I could barely see the sandbars that defined this section of river. The ribbons of current on the surface mirrored the windrows of sand on the river bottom. The water got shallower as the interval between the windrows decreased. Then, great and gentle humps of sand appeared above the water, like whales surfacing.

I paddled through sand for a week. On either side of the river were big sand dunes. The water was shallow. Under a faded denim sky, the heat unhinged the view. The dunes, already a light color, under the white sun become iridescent, as though an unsatisfied watercolorist had given the paper a rinse. A bird, too far away to identify, a dark spot on the water, was just enough to keep Loon going forward.

The heat made me lazy. I would rather have been swimming than paddling. I pulled to the side of the river, gliding the last ten feet, looking forward to the gentle hiss as bow bites sand. The bugs danced in the air around me without intent. I stripped.

The whiteness of my body surprised me. My hands, up to the wrists, were nut brown. Inside my boots my feet had taken a beating. They were smelly, chafed from portaging, and blistered. I poked at the red spots on the big toes and on the anklebone. My feet looked like an old man's, white, red, and wrinkled, with viny, wine red blood vessels inside the arch.

The water in the shallows was warm. I sat down in it and lay back. I looked at my toes sticking up across the water from my head. Out in the current the temperature was about 39°F. If I fell in there, I would have about fifteen minutes before it sucked the heat out of my bones. Then, I would turn blue.

I thought of my friend Aki, from Japan. We have never met, but we correspond. He is a solo canoeist, too. He has come from Tokyo for the past six years and has taken three-month-long trips each time. He does not shoot any rapids. He walks around them all, but that does not mean he stays out of harm's way.

In his letter last winter, he included an arresting short paragraph. On last summer's journey, he had stopped at an island, beached his kayak on the upriver side, and walked to the island's downriver end to scout the rapids below. Standing there, he watched his kayak float by with everything in it, even his small emergency radio. There was no food on the island. He would be eaten by the bugs. He had no way to get to shore. Without hesitating he threw himself in the water and swam for the kayak. He reached it, but had no strength left. He lost consciousness and woke up on shore with the kayak, not knowing how he had gotten there. It was this sentence I will never forget: "I saw the surface of the water from under the water." And he was back out here somewhere this summer.

I soaped up on the beach and returned to the water to rinse. When you're wet the bugs do not land on you. Getting out, I slid a foot through my underwear, trying not to get sand in. This is hard to do standing on one foot, and I went hopping down the beach. Dressed, I pushed Loon off, climbed over the packs, slipped out the paddle, and began again.

The dimple swirls of my paddle strokes disappeared behind Loon, unwinding after each repetitive up-and-down stroke, stitching me deeper and deeper into the fabric of the water and the land. The islands, even the sandflats, obscured the river ahead. It was difficult to tell where the main channel ran. I came to a long view. I tried to match it up with the map. I drifted. The sand under the canoe had a delicious amber color. The hot weather and the still air made Loon the only ripple maker, except for the tiny insects struggling on the water's surface.

To the sides and ahead of Loon's bow wave, the rocks meeting the water at the shore visually repeated themselves on top of the water. Piles of rock, no matter how long and tall, make shell images, each half, the other's perfection, compressing to a dark line where the two halves meet. If I looked back when Loon's wake reached shore, the shell's lower half dispersed in ripples, like smoke.

For the last five miles, I paddled toward a high, flesh-colored bluff. Banks of cloud had been moving in from the southwest. They floated free of one another, their bottom edges darker than their tops. There was a lot of moisture in the air; it would rain, but probably not today.

It was a high bluff, indicated as an island on the map, not far from the mainland. An isthmus of land ran out toward the island from a large line of granite hills marching in from the west, the first solid stone I had seen in days. I lost and crossed the main channel several times on my way in.

I set up the tent and straightened things at camp before I climbed the bluff for a look around. There were

Inuit tent rings on top, circles of stones. The grass had grown over each rock, embedding them. In use the rocks would have sat on an edge of skin, or canvas, holding it down. Finding tent rings, or any artifact, makes me smile, but now also fills me with a sadness. The Inuit no longer live on the land as they did for centuries, not since the 1950s. People say, and most Inuit agree, that is just fine.

Some people say there are still Inuit living on the land. They are called Tunit, or "Little People," who stay well out of sight, or maybe they are "Big People." There is not universal agreement about their size, but you hear stories of the descendants of the race of Inuit before the present-day Inuit. People have seen footprints. Old landmarks have been dismantled in out-of-the-way places, seemingly for no reason. People say the Tunit have always been there—even in the old days, keeping their distance. They did not care, or even hear, when the Canadian government called, "All-y, All-y, Income Free."

Maybe it is not Tunit, but a few modern Inuit families, say some of those who used to live in the Garry Lakes, who still survive quietly on the land, who choose not to come in. Maybe they maintain a few discreet contacts with one or two non-gossiping hunters in Coppermine, or Baker Lake, who slip them things they can use, like knives, needles, thread, hooks, line.

What would you do if you found one of these people? After all, they are entitled to the benefits of modern medicine, education, and welfare that the government provides other natives. What would you do? Turn them in? Not tell anybody?

I used my binoculars to look north, to see what lay ahead tomorrow. More sand and a wider river. Somewhere ahead, Pelly Lake. Then I looked inland. The granite hills were inviting. Maybe I should walk away from the river here.

I scanned the beach on the isthmus and a small pond behind it, returning to look again at a white mass to the right of the beach in the grass. I could not make it out.

I looked at the water where fifty geese were swimming away from the beach. I could barely see their silhouettes. The ripples in the water, the inverted "Vs" flowing out behind them, were what gave the geese away.

Fixing dinner, I thought about that white thing. Maybe I would take a look. I wanted to read, not having done any in a while. I bring long French novels on my trips. In this one, Esmeralda had just been snatched from the murderous crowd by the hunchback, and I wanted to know what happened next. I started to read but put the book down.

I pushed Loon in empty. She moved on tiptoe, barely touching the water. We skimmed along the edge of the island, headed for the beach. I could not find the white mass I had been looking at. It happens that way. You think you see something special, and before you get there, it changes into something ho-hum.

I was about to turn back. I saw it. How unusual! The carcass of a musk-ox. I approached it slowly. What was left of the body lay prostrate, head and chest pointing north. It was big. The skull and chest cavity still had skin and some wool on them. No real meat was left, but it had not been dead long. The body was evaporating slowly. The skin was dark leathery stuff, more like a starched fabric draped casually over the bones, each rib and vertebra clearly showing through.

On the ground around the skeleton were large clumps of woolly hair, light and dark umber brown. There was a lot of kiviat, the underwool, soft as cashmere. Only flies and bits of the wool moved in the light wind. The wool wavered like small flames, or like dandelion seeds before they are launched by the wind.

I went around to the front to admire the horns. They were light brown, deeply furrowed at their base where they emerged from the skull, and wide. They curved along the side of the skull, each horn the mirror image of the other, tapering to a point that was almost black. The right horn was broken off three inches from the tip. I could saw off the good horn. It would make a good souvenir. That is what I decided to do. I would come back in the morning.

That night I thought about the musk-ox. Was it a he or a she? How did it die? Where I come from many of us die of old age. We often get to choose where we want to die, or at least where we want to be buried.

My friend Jack, an older Inuk, says the musk-ox is

king in the tundra. Most people think the bear is. Jack says not much bothers either one, but what makes the musk-ox king is that it's peaceful, not aggressive the way the bear can be.

In the morning, I made lunch, found the saw, a piece of string to measure distance with, and a notebook: a day of field research. I would measure what I could, check the teeth, try to determine the age and sex. I had a "study" that would stay in one place.

Unlike in a jungle or a forest, nothing rushes in to cover over what dies in the tundra. Bones can lie on the ground for years, getting whiter and whiter. But the tundra is good in its own way at hiding things, although it seems so open. The tundra asks, can you find something you were not already prepared to see?

By the afternoon, I had worked a great deal on the musk-ox, even though there was not a great deal of musk-ox to work on. The skeleton's length, the size of the skull, and the worn condition of the teeth indicated it was old. I had not cut off the horn in the morning. Maybe the musk-ox had been working, too. When I began to cut the horn, I could not do it. Something held me back, seemed wrong. Other animals had "disrupted the integrity" of its body; why shouldn't I? But I decided to wait, to think about it. If I wanted the horn that badly, I could come back in Loon after I had packed up.

I did not take down my tent. Back at camp, I wondered if in all my measuring and poking I had really looked at the musk-ox. Maybe my "observing" was not complete. I began to wonder about the creatures that had taken a part of it, fed on him. I decided to go back.

Two days later, I was still there. This is stupid, I kept telling myself. Look at what you are doing. If I tell anyone I spent three days looking at a dead musk-ox, they will think I am nuts.

A wolf watched me the afternoon of the third day, as I walked ever-widening circles around the body. The wolf sat on the small dune behind the beach for at least half an hour, watching. Absorbed in what I was doing, I didn't see it leave. I was trying to find as many bones as I could. Not that I wanted to put the musk-ox back together again, but I thought the scattered bones might suggest how many animals, and what kind, had taken part of the beast. I found leg bones two hundred yards away, picked clean. To move them would have taken a wolf, a wolverine, or a bear. Since the skeleton was mainly intact, a bear probably hadn't found the kill. A bear would have smashed it up. I found other bones, some with tiny gnaw marks. A ground squirrel, or maybe a mouse, had gnawed on the bones for calcium. I found parts of the musk-ox within a circumference equal to a New York City block and several farther afield.

Sawing off the horn reminded me of souvenirs I had seen in people's homes. That was what my horn desire was a part of, to declare to myself and to impress others that I had been to the tundra. Our museums are full of this desire, protected under the wing of science, and we still operate as though objects have no spirit. No wonder native people are calling on our great museums to return their belongings and bones.

I turn on the TV and watch nature programs, electronically tidied up, without sweat or danger. The camera's lens brings my eye right up to the tiniest details, all set to music. The novelist Colette, in her collected journals, *The Earthly Paradise*, tells how, as a woman in her eighties, rich in a lifetime of feelings and of observing the natural world, she was taken to see her first movie, a nature film produced by Walt Disney. She watched the trap-door spider catch its prey in the desert of Arizona. Through time-lapse cinematography she watched a rose grow from a seed, bloom, and then die and have its petals blown away—all within two minutes. She saw polar bears on the arctic ice kill seals. All this she saw without leaving Paris. After she had described the film in loving detail in her journal, she closed by saying it was a sorry day for the human imagination.

That night I put down more of my woolly thoughts. My ten-year-old nephew, Marshal, asked me to write him a letter from the tundra. Over the summer I had been making him an alphabet of things around me. "A" is for arctic, "B" is for bear, that kind of thing. I called it a Tundrabet. The entries were short because I had only a small amount of paper. That night I wrote the letter "M."

"M" is for Marshal, also for musk-ox. Let me tell Marshal about the musk-ox. If you haven't seen one, you wouldn't believe they exist. They seem out of a myth. Nietzsche tells us how the gods killed themselves when one of their number claimed there could be only one god and one god only: they died laughing. Science and monotheism have driven the gods from Olympus but not the musk-ox from the arctic. The technician is the modern missionary bringing every bird, every grass blade, wave pattern, and molecule into the fold of human knowledge and domination. As we continue to unfurl our presence on earth, must everything have a name and a use?

For the fourth day in a row, I visited him. I thought "him" now. The technically correct "it" used when referring to animals did not make sense any longer. My initial reaction to the carcass had been to cut the horn off. Now, I saw how much life had come from his death. Along with the half dozen possible animal beneficiaries, there would have been birds. Definitely the seagull. Maybe a raven. I found a small nest, a hundred yards from the body, partially lined with musk-ox kiviat.

I looked more closely at his carcass. There were flies. Under the skull was a colony of small, jet black beetles that scattered into the grass when I turned the skull over. When I left that afternoon, I noticed in the low-angled sunlight a density of spiderwebs in the grass around the musk-ox. Spiders were using him as bait.

The Inuit's view of immortality was different from that of the first Europeans they met. The Europeans believed the soul was immortal, and the body was disposable. The Inuit the first Europeans met believed the body was immortal. The Inuit could see it was immortal in the life around them. They killed animals. They lived in a sea of blood, ate the flesh of what they killed. They used the hides for shelter and clothing, the bones for tools. They watched all forms of life eat and be eaten. Every creature lived on through the one that ate it, until it was eaten. All the feeding went back to the earth. Understanding this cycle gave the Inuit a sense of reverence and continuity.

I loaded Loon that evening and paddled one last time to the small beach to say good-bye, or thank you, or something like that. In returning, I realized one more creature nourished by the musk-ox: myself.

I had come to know this spot by walking it. I knew the feel of the grass, the curves of the land, the beach where the wolf sat and watched me, where the small nest was lined with the kiviat. I had given my full attention.

Three

Afterlife

Lightning. A storm coming. I see it in the distance, a far-off turbulence. Lightning again, and one sharp thunderclap. The western sky is dark, slab-like, cut down the middle by another lightning flash. The low morning sun in the east highlights the black storm front, ending in the sawtooth tops of faraway pines. I come around the side of the house and see the tree, now a year later, in late August leaf. The field around it is kneedeep in grass, turned straw. The lawn leading to the field is cut short; green grass flowing from the house to melt into the field around the huge oak where it stands alone. I've felt at sea most of this last year, adrift. And you? There are too few navigational aids, aren't there, Rene?

I am drawn back to the tree. When we were here, Rene, we were happy. Wind touches the tall grass, ruffles its way through the field, the way I tousle Sam's hair. I hear the wind in the needles of the white pines near our friends' house, a protective whisper compared to its harsher rustle through the leaves of the huge red oak. The tree is more than four hundred years old; its thick lower branches swing out. Several pillow on the earth, then rise; odd, horizontal waves of wood, limbs as large around as the trunks of other oaks stand upright. At some point it had been young, seeking its own light among taller trees, twisting and reaching up. Its young efforts mark its shape and must have helped it survive. When it became a mature tree, people must have savored its shade to picnic under, or rest their teams of oxen or horses. No one cut it down. It's a tough and lucky old tree. I watch the wind flip clusters of its leaves up, exposing their lighter green undersides.

I've come to tell the tree it failed us. It's our anniversary, not of our wedding under the tree but of the day you died. Emotions are no more visible than the wind, until they touch something.

We didn't want the single point of a church steeple. We came under the tree for its multiple spires of unordered order, with a taproot sunk equally deep in the earth. I look around. There is nothing out of place here. How could there be, it's nature. Nature. I'd like to kick the tree. The red oak presides. Cicadas pick up each other's cry, raising their long, dry trill from different trees, then tapering it off: CHICcceee. And again. CHICC-ceeeeeee. More than anything, I've hated nature this year. And I had built my life around her, loved her as much as I loved you, Rene. Then, suddenly, you're gone, and she killed you.

Sam has bounded ahead, off to the side, into the tall grass. I turn my head and spit. At least Sam is enjoying himself. I want the tree to hear what this year's been like, and it can't talk back.

Sam barks. Rene, was it a week or ten days before you died that you said to me, to soften what we knew was coming, "Don't worry. I'll be around. You can't fall out of the universe."

I remember the evening you died. The cancer had spread to your lungs: August 17. Your death is still hard, impossible to accept. I don't sense the terrain getting any easier. There will never be more of you, even if what you said is true.

You had chosen not to take another palliative treatment, shots of platinum directly into your blood. The doctors said they would always have another treatment to offer. We tried many, holistic as well as standard and often horribly rigorous western ones: lumpectomy, radiation, and chemotherapy. You were a psychologist, familiar with the fear you had to face. Then you became the one in the mirror, not the one in front of it directing action but the subject of nature's logic, if you can call such cruelty logic.

I don't want to go down to the tree. Why did I come back? What's gained? Getting mad at a tree makes as much sense as bumping into you on the street, although

I've caught myself thinking I hear your voice or see you just going through a door. What clues will I find? I'm a broken record, going over it all again and again.

I'm scared. And I'm tired. I've been running from things long enough. We told each other one night what it was like facing death. I'd done it time and again, in nature's face, for the fun of it, traveling alone, months at a time in the arctic: bears, rapids, a broken leg, one mistake and life's over. I loved it, found it exciting, an edge to walk. I always felt nature was on my side. You said you found aspects of your illness exciting, sometimes, but you would never have asked to go on the journey if you'd been given a choice. We did not know the outcome either, not at first. This was just something to go through.

There was this difference: over those two and a half years of illness, you were going toward your fears, making death, who never was a stranger, more a friend. In all my traveling I was really going away from my fears, keeping things simple, avoiding complexity. You explained it to me once as though you were turning from a fraction into a whole number: you drew it out for me, $1/4$ into $4/1$. You said, see, everything is the same, but if you face your fear, you stop being a fraction. This was happening even while the cancer whittled away at your body.

By last year's late June, you were losing weight and tired; it was hard for you to breathe. The cough we heard first in the winter was stronger. Climbing stairs, any stairs, became difficult. You had to pause, catch your breath, furious you could not act your age— thirty-five. The last time we saw your oncologist you asked him how much time he had seen platinum add. He said not more than nine months. You asked him about the side effects. He said pretty grim. You thanked him without comment. In the car, you said you wouldn't do it, not just to live a little longer. After that, we got ready, not believing or knowing what for.

I turn around, looking for Sam. He is way down by the woods. From here to the tree is a short distance but the longest journey, Rene. There is no narration in death. It's bizarre. People act strange.

After you died, Sam and I spent an hour with you. There was no room in our apartment for us that night. Your family wanted to stay there. Nat slept on the couch and Kate in the spare bedroom. Peter went to his wife and children, who were staying nearby. Your mother wanted to sleep in the bed with you. She did until, in the early morning, "voices" told her to leave the room. You worried most about her, the effect your dying would have on her.

I drove across the river, headed to what was to be our new home, but I could only drive up and down beside the silent, deserted, black water. The river, darker than the sky, was more threatening than anything I remember seeing. I love rivers, but that night saw only dark relentlessness. Another of nature's magic tricks: take a bright, beautiful, blue river, cover it with darkness. . . . take a beautiful, young woman . . .

An odd piece of trivia surfaced in me: the "Thames" of the River Thames means "the dark one." That could be any river, even the Charles River in Boston. Driving, I thought what had just happened couldn't have happened, not in Boston. Death happened in exotic places like Paris, China, Rome. In novels. In the newspaper. In other people's lives, somewhere else, anywhere else, and not to you, not to me. NO.

I drove slowly, trying to focus, feeling the breeze along the left side of my face, along my bare arm resting out the window. I watched the river. I could not see it moving, but I knew it was; it had to be. I drove upriver, then turned around and drove back down along Memorial Drive. "The dark one." I drove slowly. I looked past Sam, who sat beside me framed by the window. We were both in a daze.

I had come into the bedroom. You were propped on the pillows. You'd been in a coma all day. Your heart was racing at the same time as your pulse began to slow down. The two can only diverge for so long before they have to stop. You were so thin. In the kitchen, your family was eating. A joke had just been told. Laughter ran through the apartment, easing their tension.

I turned to call Sam, turned back to you. In between, you changed. Or I thought you had. I was by you in a second. Did I feel your heart's last flutter? You were warm, but nothing moved. I closed your eyes. In the kitchen, I said to Peter (I had to tell someone specific) that it had happened, you had died. We were all beside you, touching you. You lay on your back. Nat threw open the window. Your front was cool, but there was still heat underneath you, along your spine. Sam jumped on the bed, licked your hand, your face; sniffed you all over. You didn't move. I held your hand.

July and August had been so hot. We'd get up at night, if your breathing became difficult, to stand in front of the air conditioner, to lean into it resting our hands on our thighs, letting our mouths come close to the cold air, our naked shoulders touching. It was easier for you to breathe the cold air up close. We would imagine ourselves as two large salmon nosing their way forward in a cold current, except ours was made of air. We'd describe to each other the slow undulations of their great bodies. Their slow moving gills. Their instinct to keep going.

I drove to our home on Hawthorn Street. Buying it, fixing it up, had been a bright note in contrast to the dark visits to the doctors. The renovations were complete. There was a cot, the only furniture in the house, but I could not sleep. I felt as hollow, as empty, as the house.

My griefs, whatever they had been, fit in my body. They were manageable. Now, I walk an odd terrain, as if I am a small particle dwarfed by grief, the world a reckless geography. They don't tell you how quiet the terrain is. I expected a hurricane, a tornado, a tidal wave, an earthquake—all the plagues that range the world destroying. I expected to feel as though I were in one, or all of them at once. But I didn't. It's more as it appears after the fact, the city destroyed, crops wasted, houses wrecked. It happens in silence. I can walk around the house, pick things up (your things), and be destroyed: no hurricane wind necessary.

Your last trip away from bed was to inspect the work at the house. Peter helped me carry you downstairs to the car in your wheelchair. You loved being outside, driving by the river, blue under the hot August sun, feeling the breeze on your cheek. I pushed the wheelchair through the freshly painted rooms, around all that empty, renovated space. The floors glistened. We had realized in July, only months after our wedding, that our hopes for a long life together would not come true, that the effort for you to move into our home would be too much. Better to stay where you knew everything, where everything was on one level, close by.

Even so, 18 Hawthorn Street became our home. You enjoyed thinking about it, looking at the pictures of the work, directing my efforts. You were happy to think of it as the place where Sam and I would live, a place for our two families to gather. You had provided it, for all of us, as a strong gesture of family. The day we toured the house, on the second floor, you asked me to lean down and said softly, how lovely it all was, how sad you were.

I remember the Sunday we first saw the house, a few days after our wedding. We had nothing more than our broker's call, saying there is a house that has just come on the market. For a year, he had helped us look for a home, one roof to cover our lives. We were accustomed to disappointment and went without expectation.

As the owner's broker opened the door, he said, "How unusual. Your name is Perkins, and so was the name of the family who owned the house." The house had belonged to a distant cousin, one I'd never met. He had died eight years before. His widow had died at ninety-two a month before we saw the house. Fate? It was a beautiful old Victorian home, spacious and comfortable. No lawn to mow. We felt at home in it. We were the first couple to see it. By the end of the day, four couples wanted it.

We were lucky. The evening we signed the papers, I carried you over the threshold. Sam burst in ahead of us, skidding on the bare, hardwood floors. We brought a miniature bowling set, wooden pins, and two small wooden bowling balls. We set the pins up at one end of the first floor and bowled from the other. Sam chased the balls, made sure all the pins were knocked over.

We kissed in each room of the house.

The last time we talked about the house, you hoped Sam and I would move in. You worried we would not because it was too big, too sad. I said we would. You were happy, ran your feet up over the wall at the head of the bed and said you'd come and visit. It made you feel good to know where we'd be. You said it helped fill in the map of your future.

A hawk glides into my view, rising up from behind the oak tree, effortless wing against a black sky, compressed wind made visible. It screes before giving itself to the wind, sliding off to where its circling began. I look around for Sam. He's bounding through the field, still looking for something, sniffing.

A sight like the hawk used to thrill me. Now, that hawk seems part of someone else's life, someone I used to know. I close my eyes. I squeeze them and see stars, galaxies, constellations with black space between them. Lots of black space, a mass of bright dots—God's salt. Your mother is the astrologer, she knows the stars and her way around them. She believes in pendulums, healers, and the cutting edge of New Age insight. When we met she offered to do my chart. I thought that would be great, but you suggested that I might want to keep that private.

I wanted your mother to like me. I wanted you to get better. I wanted to return to the tree together, again and again. I wanted. I would not make a good Buddhist; too many wants. There are unhappy endings, and there are people who do not like me.

I'll wait for Sam to tire out, then we'll leave. There's no reason to go down to the tree. I'll just sit here. I've been so tired. What could this tree tell me that I can't see from here? How can I be mad at it? It's just a tree. It's my memories and what has happened that I'm furious about. Since the memories won't go away, I let them keep rolling through me, clouds across the sky.

In November I did see a hawk that moved me, a red-tail. I was sitting at my desk when I heard crows, lots of them. I ran outside. Often, an owl, a hawk, or even a cat can set them off. Nothing out front but raucous crows. Out back, in the neighbor's tree, the hawk. It sat on a low branch, soaking in the early morning sun, in profile, not more than twenty feet away. I said, I'll stay until you go. There it sat, preening, the feathers on its head fluffing out each time it bent its neck. All around, the black crows cawed, hopped from branch to branch. The hawk, oblivious, acted as though they were not there.

I realized it was you, come to visit. I would stay until you left. I was still there forty minutes later. Sam was worrying a bone back and forth over the driveway. I could hear his teeth grinding on the bone, the bone scratching along the pavement. A few yellow leaves still clung to the maple tree, between them the bluest sky. The hawk would pick up a claw, scratch her head. At one point, I scratched my jaw, felt the bone under the skin.

Later that week, I asked an ornithologist why crows dislike hawks. They don't eat them, or kill them, the way owls do. Not able to think of any practical reason other than territory, he looked up and said, "Maybe they're just like that."

I did not get to know another side of your mother until we were married. The day after our wedding, we were driving to Manchester for lunch with my parents. As we reached the Mystic River Bridge in heavy traffic, she leaned forward from the back seat to tell us that, in Atlanta, she had asked her psychic to do a reading of you, to tell her what he saw concerning your cancer. She said he hesitated, since he did not like doing readings without the subject present, but for her he relented. He said he saw a great blackness around you. That this was the cancer. He said that, I, Rob had given it to you. That it was something you would have to work out.

I remember my knuckles were white as I gripped the steering wheel. In the front seat, we were both silent. Finally, you turned to her and said, "You cannot say that. It is irresponsible to even think it." She sat back in her seat and said, "I didn't say it. My psychic did."

Through your reading you knew from the writing of Elisabeth Kübler-Ross about the different stages of grieving. There are five: denial, rage, blame, bargaining, and finally, with luck and work, acceptance. You helped me understand them, and that night you said your mother's remarks came from the third stage. That we shouldn't be surprised by anyone's reactions, even our own, in the face of your illness.

I've read C. S. Lewis's book *A Grief Observed* more than once. It's polished, full of mature thought about loss, but I am more satisfied by music. Until this year, I was indifferent to symphonies. But after your death, a friend in New York sat me down in front of her speakers, put on the Brahms Requiem, and listened with me. Since then, that piece, and other music, has grown on me, has filled the places words cannot reach. But I've had little of this calmness. I've often felt more like the figure in Munch's *The Scream* than anything else.

In December, I went to make the apartment "broom clean" for the new owner. Everything had been taken away—by your family, by friends, by me. I came to clean. I had broom, bucket, mop, vacuum. I pushed the dust around, filled two bags with small things to throw away—all the unnoticed bits and dirt that had lived with us stuck in corners, in cupboards. I mopped and swept. I looked out the windows for the last time. It was a sunny day. Inside, the light caught the dust, creating bright shafts in the room. The dust swam slowly in them.

"You can't fall out of the universe."

Last fall, I often sat on the front steps at 18 Hawthorn Street, lethargic, listening to acorns falling. In the pin oak out front, squirrels were at work. You'd be surprised at the different sounds a falling acorn makes. The noise is a loud, metallic "bonk" on a car. Landing on the pavement or in the grass, an acorn makes a duller sound. Several plunked on the wooden stairs beside me, and one bounced off my head, making a hollow plonk, the way something heavy would sound dropped on a rock under water.

The fallen acorns stood out like stars against the new, black-painted steps. I stared hard at them. I saw the smooth, brown shell, how the sun shadow appears as the nut skin curves around itself, how the dimpled, light brown cap fits on the shell, and how sharp a yellow the cap is at its tip. In the street, the breeze blew the brown leaves around. They scratched along the pavement making dry, stiff sounds, not the soft velvet rustle of the spring leaves we heard when we first came to the house. I'd sit there on the steps thinking, who cares?

I just plain ached. People seemed odd to me. They wandered by chatting, roller-blading, holding hands. I could not help thinking of them as corpses. It was hard to sleep, even to lie prone. It scared me. I might not wake up.

One Sunday, I finished two fried eggs, bacon, butter and jam on two hard rolls. I remember thinking: I am still alive. I've just eaten breakfast.

Afterlife. I never wholly believed in it, but I do now. There is life after death, but not the way I imagined. Afterlife is what happens to us here, to me. It is after life. It's not about you. I entered it the night you died. Numb and confused, I float, wander like smoke, blown in any which way.

Tell me there's more. As you believed, are you back in the world? Where are you back in the world?

People, your family, my family, say to me (I say it to myself): "You died well, at peace. You are an inspiration to us." True as that is, you're gone. I can't imagine the adventures you are on.

Sam misses you. He leaps at our friends, especially women. The other day I said hello to a neighbor as she got out of her car. Sam bolted across the street toward the sound of her hello. If I hadn't had the leash on, he would have been hit by a passing car.

One night, not sleeping, lying beside you, listening to the water in the oxygen tube gurgle as your thin breaths came and went, I could not imagine how you felt anymore. I lay on my back and two lines of single tears ran down the sides of my face, into my ears. I felt like Gulliver tied down, a giant pinned by these little things, by these two tiny lines of tears. Then, the gurgles stopped. The harder I listened, the less I heard. Tense, I strained to hear you breathe. It's all about breath, isn't it? I thought, God, Rene, you've died. What do I do? Do I let you rest, let you go on your way for the night, and tell your family in the morning? Paralyzed, unable to make up my mind, I must have fallen asleep because the next thing I knew you'd jabbed me in the ribs and said to roll over, stop snoring! I was never happier.

Falling in love, years earlier, coming back from an expedition, I met you at Nat's cabin in Maine. I loved that the cabin was secluded at the far side of your family's island. It was deep summer, everything humming. The blue sea circled the island, green spruces scratched the blue sky, and white sand and hard rocks edged the shore. We had no running water and kept a bucket upstairs near the bed for washing ourselves: the sweat off our bodies and all the luscious fluids that poured from them. This was nothing to do with family or friends. We sat on the beach and baked. Then swam. Then ate. Then loved. You wore a wide-brimmed straw hat that hid everything but your big, white smile. The wind circled sweetly through everything, including us, blowing back the brim of that ridiculous, wide-brimmed straw hat, revealing brown eyes.

One afternoon, we found a little stream draining a swamp. We sat side by side on the log at the edge of the swamp enjoying our two bodies in the sun. We said it would be good to come back at night, like going to the movies.

We returned to sit on the old, crumbling log that evening. Our arrival made the swamp silent. We felt foolish sitting in the dark. Slowly, we saw things and heard sounds that had been there all the time: the stream in front of our feet, the crescent beach a hundred yards away, where each wave was a breath mixing thousands of sand grains with each receding wave. The small, dark shapes of fiddler crabs darted back and forth across the stream. We said little. We sat watching, waiting.

The colorful details that hold the eye in daylight were absent. In their place substance appeared as it was: mass and volume, dark, secret, unrevealed, hinted at—a fundamental landscape. Even in this darkness were darker pockets, as if some primal parts of the world had not yet been assigned a role, or colored in.

Occasionally, we heard dry grass crackle, a twig snap. Once a bat flew over our heads. We heard the hooting of a great horned owl. To us, the brook became orchestra to this night theater. This was nature that entertained and thrilled, even knowing the darkness was full of the fear of creatures who foraged at night and those that hunted them. We sat on the log. We had each other. What we watched couldn't touch us.

A cruel annunciation, Rene. To be told you had a malignant tumor, and not a small one. Breast cancer. You stood at the sink. I sat at the table. You turned, saying that the biopsy had proved positive, that you'd fight this with all you had. That was what you were going to do. What would I do? I said, I'm your companion wherever we're going. Then we were in each other's arms.

You told me later, after that pronouncement, even on good days, you felt you traveled through a darker world, one more like that night swamp we watched in Maine. I felt it, too, and shrank from the grass, the trees, the shrubs. The cancer was part of nature. In the tundra, she has threatened my life. But this. I thought: the grass, the trees, they are all growing like your tumor.

The odd thing at the house is that I receive mail for four Perkinses, and three of them are dead. It just comes through the slot. Mr. Perkins died eight years ago, and he gets more catalogs and fund-raising appeals than any of us. If I died, I am sure the mail would keep coming through the slot, filling up the whole house.

I put the ring in a small box and the box in a sock. It was the engagement ring my father gave my mother in San Francisco during the war. As I remember the story, they met at a dinner party. My dad liked her, wanted to ask her out. All he knew was her last name, Cushing. He called all the Cushings in the phone book until he found one with a daughter, Flo. Standing in the phone booth, he asked her if she'd like to go to a particular play. My mother said that she'd seen it. Awkward silence. Not knowing what to say next, he said good-bye and hung up. He bought a paper, looked up another show, and called her back. This time she said she would love to go. Whether she'd seen that show before, or not, I never heard.

After dinner, I pulled out the sock. As I handed it to you, Sam jumped up, grabbed it, and ran into the other room. I said, "You might like to get it back. It's for you."

Do I keep you close by trying to hold on to every memory? Or would I keep you closer by letting go? I can't unpuzzle this. Everything I misplace or can't find or forget, even a phone number, is another loss that makes me cry.

The hospitals kept getting larger, the treatments more expensive, the machinery bigger, as if inadequate human efforts could be masked by these cold technologies. At the same time, we saw healers who offered simple solutions. Boston's leading macrobiotic healer said that if you followed his diet faithfully, you would be cured in nine months. Then he said a year. On our last visit to his center in Brookline, we let him diagnose you before we told him you had a recurrence. He pronounced you cured. After we left, we cried. It's fair to say that the doctors, none of them, have answers, or guarantees, and the best of them admit it.

I do not wish to move an inch from our shared life, but I am pulled relentlessly forward by the days.

Trying to heal an eye tumor, we went with your mother to Massachusetts General Hospital to see an expert. We took courage from the scale of the place, the way suppliants must have felt entering cathedrals in the Middle

Ages. We took more courage from seeing we were the youngest people in the waiting room. We were confident. The doctor was the expert. We waited an hour. We waited two. We did not mind. We were asked to talk with his nurse. She interviewed you. She asked a litany of questions as though she had something else on her mind. You answered concisely. You had gotten good at this, too. Bored, I looked at the nurse, trying to imagine how she enjoyed doing this every day. She wore a hot pink skirt under her white lab coat. She wore white high heels. She asked the questions. You answered.

We took a seat again in the waiting room. We would have blood drawn, a standard test the nurse said, but we would see the doctor first. We saw him. He could not speak English well. He said very little. He was Greek. He nodded thoughtfully to the questions we asked. Two assistants took notes. He had fifteen minutes for us, enough time to prescribe treatment. Actually, the assistant prescribed the treatment later. All the time, your mother kept telling him, and us, how she could tell he was a great doctor. That he was a spiritual man, that he had a good aura.

We went to a lower floor to have the blood drawn. The kind, older nurse, sympathetic about the thinness of your veins, knew how hard it was for you to suffer one more needle. She made it as easy as she could. We should have asked before, but we asked afterwards, what the test was for. She said it was a test for pregnancy. You had had your ovaries removed months ago as part of the campaign to reduce your estrogen levels. You had told this to the blonde nurse. Now nervous, the older nurse said maybe it was a test for something else. Upstairs you asked the other nurse why she had ordered the blood drawn. She said to check for pregnancy. You screamed at her that you had no ovaries. That you had told her that. Calmly, she replied that she interviewed more than thirty patients a day and that mistakes happen. We shouldn't blame her.

At lunch in the cafeteria, we took our trays to an empty table, exhausted. Your mother repeatedly said how impressed she was with the doctor's aura. There wasn't much to say, except to agree with her that he was a good man, really good, and wise.

The Greek doctor, the expert, entered the cafeteria, tray in hand. He passed his eye over us on his way to a table of doctors. They made room for him. They wore white coats. It was odd having just seen him, confided in him, put our trust in him, not to have him acknowledge us. He didn't even sit up straight. The other doctors stopped eating when he spoke. There was laughter. We could not stop watching him. After all, he sees a lot of patients; even doctors have to eat, and when an expert speaks, people listen.

How many alphabets of emotion did we experience?

At night, the Cambridge Common is where Sam and I walk. No one goes there. We have the streets and the common to ourselves. People are fearful of being mugged, robbed, or murdered. To confront a man who wished to harm me would give me pleasure, a chance to meet someone at my level of intensity. It would be amusing. I don't feel fearful, Rene. Not now. Quietly, in a calm voice, I would explain that whatever the threat was it had no sting, not compared to our experience. I wonder if my words would be met with disbelief, or a shrug, or a bullet. If I were killed, fine. I'd be wherever you are sooner.

I forget so much these days. I walked to the car and saw the gas cap on the roof, wedged under the roof rack. I thought, who's been siphoning gas? In the car, the gauge read full. Then I remembered I had filled the tank two days before. I had forgotten to replace the gas cap. I almost burned the house down in November. I put bread in the toaster and wandered off. The toast never popped up, and the whole house filled with smoke. I was lucky the cabinet above the toaster hadn't burst into flame before I ran back in.

Confined to bed, you asked me to tell you how things were between your mother and me. When I told you, you leaned back on the pillows and said it sounded like a soap opera to you. You said that you and she would talk.

A few days later, in the evening, she and I were having a drink with Peter in the living room. Your mother said, "Rene and I have talked about your values, and we like them. But I want you to know that I question your motives."

"What?" I asked.

"Why are you here?"

"I love Rene, and I'm her husband," I said, thinking what odd conversations we have. Shortly afterwards, she and Peter went into the kitchen. As I sat alone, it struck me what she meant. I went into the kitchen, trying to be calm, and said to her that we had to return to our conversation. "You can't say you question my motives without questioning my values. That you can't do, not without protest. It's heartless of you to imply I didn't marry Rene for love."

She made light of her remarks and, as if waving it all away, said, "We were just airing our feelings, that's all. Besides, I did not say, 'Why are you here?' I said, 'What do you do?'"

Steel I-beams would have melted under the tension between us. Standing by the refrigerator, Peter said, "No, Mother, you said, 'Why are you here?'"

You implored me to try to understand her, to forgive. Often, I would drive her back to the motel where she stayed. Hoping for common ground and a new start, several times I apologized for my part in our rough conversations, and she would say, "You should."

On the anniversary of our wedding, I planted a hawthorn tree in our garden. Called a cockspur, it's a wild tree, the crown a whirlwind of thorn and branch. It has a beautiful pink bloom, soft gray bark, and in the fall, russet leaves. Every bird, and spirit, has sanctuary in it. My mother helped pick it out. Even she was surprised by its untamed aspect. She liked it.

At Easter, I came out in the evening to water the tree. In the pitcher I had mixed some of your ashes. I poured the water around the tree's base. At first, I was shocked to see that several white bone fragments did not sink but stayed on the surface of the brown mulch. Then I liked it.

The morning after your cremation, I was to meet your mother and Kate for a ceremony in the chapel at Mount Auburn Cemetery. You wanted me to have half your ashes and your family to have the other half. We were going to say a prayer together in the chapel before taking away our urns. In those first days after you died, the tiniest things meant the world. Never to see you again.

That morning, I saw in your diary a grooming appointment for Sam. I called to let your mother and Kate know I would be a few minutes late. Your mother, who answered the phone, agreed Sam's appointment was important and said that was fine. They would wait.

It was another hot day. I put on my suit, my wedding suit, and polished my shoes. I took Sam to the groomer. My mind was clouded, but I kept moving through each hour, one step at a time. I arrived at the cemetery only a few minutes late and walked slowly to the chapel.

I thought I must be the first to arrive because I did not see your mother or Kate inside the door. I walked toward the man behind the desk, who looked up. I said I had come to meet my mother-in-law and my wife's sister. We were collecting my wife's ashes. We were going to say a prayer together in the chapel. He looked surprised and said, "They just left. She said you would come by later today."

"Is there a note?" I said.

"No," he said.

"Nothing?"

"No, they came and took their ashes and left. She said you were with the dog."

I began to shake and leaned against the wall. The man came around his desk and helped me sit in a chair. I broke open like a smashed gourd. Between sobs, I told him how important having the ceremony was, that I had thought it was important to all of us. I had looked forward to it. It took me several minutes to stop crying. The man sat behind his desk, waiting. As I stood up, wiping my eyes, he said, "I shouldn't tell you this, but I will. Don't ever tell your mother-in-law, but I gave you 60 percent of her ashes. You were her husband and I know she loved you very much."

Still dazed, I took your ashes into the chapel. I placed them beside me in the pew. Light streamed through the stained glass window, picking up the rich color of the altar's dark wood. It was quiet. The dust motes floated in shafts of light, as though I watched air, an invisibility made visible. The very light itself seemed to have centuries of experience. The stone arches and the figures, still and silent, looked down on us.

I walked into the sunlight, and the heat on my back felt good. I carried your ashes in a shoulder bag. Instead of returning to the car, we went for a walk. We walked by simple and elaborate graves. Slowly, like a falling leaf, I touched earth. There isn't anything that isn't connected to everything else, is there, Rene?

Later that morning at Trinity Church, after we had gone over your memorial service, I asked your mother why she didn't wait. She said, "I know you are a solo canoeist, and that you'd want to be alone with your Rene."

"But you didn't tell me that," I said. On the way into the church to hear the organ play parts of the music for your service, she kept hitting me on the arms and shoulder. I had to step aside, out of reach. I asked Peter, who was watching, what I could do. He shrugged, and said, "Don't take it personally. She treats all the in-laws this way."

You couldn't go to the ocean anymore. I went for you and brought back buckets of salt water with seaweed and mussels and stones in it, scooped water from them over your head above the sink or in the bathtub. I would collect the salt water on my visits to my parents. I would go to the railroad beach, park the car, and walk the tracks to the little stretch of shore. Sam had a hard time adjusting his gait to the ties. Down among the rocks, on the beach, he picked up speed, hitting the water ahead of me. I would stop, take off my shoes, roll up my pants. But the first time I didn't. My clothes never entered my head until I was standing in the water up to my thighs. I ruined a pair of good leather shoes. Twice, a train roared by on its way to Boston. Would a passenger looking out the window have any inkling of what I was doing and why?

I remember you closed your eyes and let the water run into the corners of your mouth. You'd ask for more; it tasted so good. You'd ask me to pour slowly. You did not want to dry off, but wanted to feel the crinkle of dry salt on your skin, see its odd, white color on your body. You liked licking it off. So did Sam. So did I. The bits of seaweed in the water you put on the edge of the sink to dry. When they dried, you popped the pods between your thumb and finger, sucked on the others.

You became very thin. You could hold nothing down, liquid or solid. One evening you stood at the sink supporting yourself on it, looking in the mirror. From the bathtub, I looked up at your profile, now a slender line, beautiful and terrifying. Since you had stopped treatment, your hair was growing back in. Your pubic hair was soft and short, like a young girl's. We could see the pattern in it. We watched the spiral of black hair growing back on your head. Your skin glowed marble-like, as though a fire heated it, except where the tumor showed through red and lumpy.

It's like ivy, isn't it—cancer. It grows firmly, greedy as

it slowly strangles its host. Indifferent and unrelenting, the cancer grows too slowly to be terrifying the way a car crash is, yet a thudding fear keeps pace with it. Nothing did stop its growth. Finally, smells and the taste of ice became your world.

It's important to tell your story, isn't it, Rene? We made our film for each other. It was shown in England and Canada, and later here. Many people don't understand it. It's too startling. You wanted to use it in your work when you recovered. You put in order what mattered most, got down your feelings. That's it.

We showed the film to your family. It happened to be the night before you died. You had not been able to talk for several days. That night, it was as if you'd come back and talked to us with all your grace through the film. It was as though you'd come back to tell us that you would be all right. I stayed with you in the bedroom, but we could hear our voices in the next room. We needed your help now. You'd made your peace, even with the cancer.

Numb, we had forgotten how to let go. At the end of the film, your two brothers came in the room, bawling. The three of us, three big men, held your light body in a circle of our arms.

We skate on black ice. We are flying over the smooth, dark ice. We hear cracks and booms, but we're safe. You wear your white skates. We move side by side, or hold hands and whirl, close to each other and out at arm's length. It's cold. I see the white lines the skate blades carve in the ice, clear and separate when we're apart, an inseparable tangle as we whirl together, creating a tracery of us, independent and together. Then we are three, holding hands and spinning in a circle. Your mother has joined us. She wears a skirt. We're all smiling. It feels good. Then you are gone, and just your mother and I spin, holding hands. It still feels good.

Something lands on my forehead. I twitch, open my eyes. The grasshopper jumps to my chest, then leaps clear. I rise up on my elbows, look along my body, then slowly get up and brush off the seat of my pants. I must have dozed. Rip Van Rob.

I look around. The storm is moving off. Sunlight strengthens the dark, receding clouds, occasionally there's a low roll of thunder. Sam is still off scouting.

I imagine you in the house getting ready for our wedding under this tree, dressing in a flurry of women: Kate, your mother, Carolyn, Judy, Merrie. I walked down to the tree with the minister and Tony and my father. It was a small wedding with a big party to follow. We had heard too many stories of couples remembering nothing of their wedding. We wanted to separate the two events and to savor them.

That day the clearing sky turned gray again, and a light rain began. Umbrellas were passed out. I was nervous, standing under the tree, waiting for you. Carolyn held Sam on a leash. We watched the house, waiting for you and Andrew, who had become like a father to you after your father died. The colors of the pines, the grass, the small spring flowers glowed more brightly than they would have in sunlight. The tree's wet bark glistened. I could hear the rain hit the umbrellas and felt a light spray caress my cheek. I blinked when a drop landed on my eyelid.

You appeared on the porch and paused. Andrew held a large blue umbrella, one big enough for you both. Together you glided down the steps, onto the lawn, toward the tree, toward me. In his light brown suit, wearing a darker brown fedora, Andrew seemed like an earth god. The bright umbrella was a patch of blue sky and you in your wedding dress, a white cloud traveling safe through the rain under that patch of blue sky, supported by the earth. I held my breath as you came to rest by my side.

The tree did give us its strength just by being there. We thought of it often afterwards. It must have helped many people and will help others. I feel foolish having ever doubted it. I start to walk down to it, calling Sam in.

As I near the tree, I notice a steady stream of bees leaving and returning to the tree, halfway up, just above the crotch of a large branch that sweeps down to the ground. I walk closer. During the spring, after our wedding, our lovemaking was long and delicious, full of hope. Something unspoken gave an urgency to our bodies. We were a fabulous knot, without top or bottom. Yes, it had two ends, but in between it was impossible to fathom. Our bodies talked for us. Later, the last few times we made love, gently, we were like bees, weren't we, storing up nectar for our coming journeys. You into adventures I cannot imagine; me to remain behind.

I take off my shoes. I climb on the big limb. My bare feet have a better grip on the bark. I straddle the branch, shinny toward the hive. A constant stream of bees enters and leaves the opening in the tree. This is a large slit, a feminine shape, its edges smooth bark turned back like bedcovers. I can hear a hum, a constant droning that the tree's hollowness amplifies. Inside they are beating their wings to cool the hive. I straddle the branch. I can watch the bees land on its lip before they disappear into the dark. Others come up to the edge and take off. I turn around and try to follow their flight. The bee bodies are bright spots against the dark receding storm. I follow them with my eyes until, eventually, they disappear, poof! out of sight. It's as though they are slipping through a small tear in the sky on their way back to some celestial field of flowers.

A memory appears, one I had lost, but no less real than the hive in front of me or than the bone fragment on brown mulch: our last night together. It was late, quiet. We no longer had a regular sleeping pattern. You woke me up. I turned on the light. You could only grip my hand lightly, or nod. You were so thin, tired. You wanted me to know something. I found paper, but you could not press hard enough to make the pen work. We tried different pens, then gave up. You motioned for your date and address book. I asked, is it someone I should contact?

No.

You motioned to the book. I kept turning pages.

An appointment? Here?

You kept shaking your head. On the last page, you pointed to what you had written. I read it. I leaned into you. I read it again. We touched foreheads:

Traveler, there is no path; the path is made by walking.

The bees ignore me. They are pure verb and very present, preoccupied with life, not death. I sit on the branch watching, hypnotized by the heat, the hum of the bees, that memory. To the lip of the slit, worker bees bring out the dead bees, the exhausted bees, and even bees still alive but whose wings have frayed. They push the bodies out. The dead and dying either bounce off or catch on the limb. They are heaped in front of where I sit, or they fall to earth, softly, like a leaf spinning slow circles, depending on the frayed contour of their wings. Several are brought up and pushed out each minute. All the while, a deep and solid murmur comes from the tree.